WE HAD TO BE BRAVE

Escaping the Nazis on the Kindertransport

Jewish refugee children, part of a Kindertransport from Germany, upon arrival in Harwich, England, on December 12, 1938.

ALSO BY
DEBORAH HOPKINSON

D-Day: The World War II Invasion That Changed History

*Dive! World War II Stories of
Sailors & Submarines in the Pacific*

*Courage & Defiance: Stories of Spies, Saboteurs,
and Survivors in World War II Denmark*

Titanic: Voices from the Disaster

Up Before Daybreak: Cotton and People in America

*Shutting Out the Sky: Life in the Tenements
of New York, 1880–1924*

Two Jewish refugee children, part of a Kindertransport, upon arrival in Harwich, England, on December 12, 1938.

WE HAD TO BE BRAVE

Escaping the Nazis on the Kindertransport

Deborah Hopkinson

SCHOLASTIC
FOCUS

NEW YORK

Library of Congress Cataloging-in-Publication Data
Names: Hopkinson, Deborah, author.
Title: We had to be brave : escaping the Nazis on the Kindertransport /
Deborah Hopkinson.
Description: First edition. | New York : Scholastic Focus, an imprint of
Scholastic Inc. [2020] | Audience: Ages 8-12. | Audience: Grade 4 to 6. |
Summary: "Ruth David was growing up in a small village in Germany when
Adolf Hitler rose to power in the 1930s. Under the Nazi Party, Jewish families
like Ruth's experienced rising anti-Semitic restrictions and attacks. Just going
to school became dangerous. By November 1938, anti-Semitism erupted into
Kristallnacht, the Night of Broken Glass, and unleashed a wave of violence and
forced arrests. Days later, desperate volunteers sprang into action to organize
the Kindertransport, a rescue effort to bring Jewish children to England. Young
people like Ruth David had to say good-bye to their families, unsure if they'd
ever be reunited. Miles from home, the Kindertransport refugees entered
unrecognizable lives, where food, clothes—and, for many of them, language
and religion—were startlingly new. Meanwhile, the onset of war and the
Holocaust visited unimaginable horrors on loved ones left behind. Somehow,
these rescued children had to learn to look forward, to hope. Through the
moving and often heart-wrenching personal accounts of Kindertransport
survivors, critically acclaimed and award-winning author Deborah Hopkinson
paints the timely and devastating story of how the rise of Hitler and the Nazis
tore apart the lives of so many families and what they were forced to give up in
order to save these children"—Provided by publisher.
Identifiers: LCCN 2019020130 | ISBN 9781338255720
Subjects: LCSH: Holocaust, Jewish (1939-1945)—Juvenile literature. |
Kindertransports (Rescue operations)—Juvenile literature. | Jewish
refugees—Great Britain—Juvenile literature. | Refugee children—Great
Britain—History—20th century—Juvenile literature. | Jewish
children—Great Britain—History—20th century—Juvenile literature. |
Jewish children—Germany—History—20th century—Juvenile literature. |
World War, 1939-1945—Jews—Rescue—Juvenile literature. | LCGFT:
Historical fiction.
Classification: LCC D804.34 .H67 2020 | DDC 940.53/1535083—dc23
LC record available at https://lccn.loc.gov/2019020130

For
Lisa, Liel, Lily, and Hudson
and
for all children who must wander

January 1939
Berlin, Germany

Tears kept welling up in my eyes.

Dear mother, I don't want to leave you, I don't want to lose you.

I did not know then that I would have pathetic letters from my father, written in an unsteady handwriting, his hands shaking from forced labor of building roads, and later still twenty word messages through the Red Cross from a concentration camp. I didn't know all that then, and it was just as well . . .

The day of my journey came, a gray cold early morning in January 1939. . . . The taxi we ordered did not turn up, so we went to the station by tram. Awful scenes of children and parents, little children, adolescent boys and girls, about two hundred of us. Sandwiches, cases, last minute advice, last hugs and kisses. Then we were lined up and marched to a waiting train.

Goodbye, darling parents, goodbye . . .

I never saw them again.

—MARIANNE JOSEPHY ELSLEY

Nazi propaganda postcard featuring Adolf Hitler, a swastika flag, and a member of the Sturmabteilung (SA), or storm troopers, in Munich, Germany, about 1932.

I know very well that there are millions of stories just like mine, or much more interesting than mine . . . Why do I sit down and put it on paper?

I feel that this story should stay alive, that the younger generation should know a bit about the details of this part of Jewish history and Jewish suffering and the great urge to go on, as best you can, no matter what happens.

Just as there are Jewish families in the United States who have lived here now in peace and prosperity for three or four generations, so there were four or more generations of Jews in Germany who had lived there in peace until Hitler came along and started to destroy their lives bit by bit and in the end murdered millions of them.

—RUTH SASS GLASER

Think of us.

—From the last letter of Franz Josephy,
father of Marianne Elsley, August 1944

Voices of the Kindertransport

IMAGINE GETTING ON A TRAIN AND LEAVING YOUR PARENTS AND YOUR FAMILY BEHIND. Imagine arriving in a new place, where you don't speak the language and where everything is different. People wear clothes that seem strange; the food is different too. Imagine feeling that great danger looms and threatens those you love most, yet you have no idea what might be happening to your family back home.

This is what happened to ten thousand children who escaped Nazi-occupied countries on the Kindertransport, a rescue effort that took place in 1938–1939. *Kinder* is the German word for "children," which you probably can guess from our imported word *kindergarten*, or "children's garden." In this book, Kindertransport refers both to the overall rescue effort as well as to individual transports that carried refugees. Most of the children escaped by train, although there were several transports by plane.

$\sim$

When Adolf Hitler became chancellor of Germany in 1933, life changed for Jewish children and their families. The Nazis persecuted Jewish people, creating numerous barriers to education and earning a living. In 1935, the Nazis took away their citizenship. In 1938,

Jewish children were expelled from all state-run schools in Germany. When Germany annexed Austria in March 1938, Jews there fell under Nazi power and suffered the same hardships.

At first, the Nazis' goal was to make life so unbearable that Jews would leave. But it wasn't easy to emigrate, and not everyone could do so in time. By 1941, after the start of World War II, Hitler's "Final Solution" meant that Jews were deported to concentration camps to face almost certain death. Six million Jewish men, women, and children were murdered by the time the war ended in Europe in May 1945. Historians estimate about one million Jewish children were killed. The Nazis also targeted LGBTQ people, political prisoners, people with disabilities, and other "non-Aryan" minorities, such as those of Romany heritage.

The Kindertransport effort spared ten thousand children, primarily from Germany and Austria, from this fate. While some Kindertransport survivors have passed away, others are now in their eighties or nineties. They are active and curious citizens of the world who greet each day as a gift. Today, many continue to educate others about the Holocaust and speak out about the plight of refugees in the twenty-first century.

In putting together this book, I was inspired by many people, including Kindertransport survivor

Alfred "Freddie" Traum, who grew up in Vienna, Austria, where he sang in a Jewish boys' choir. He described his last Hanukkah performance before he and his sister left for England on the Kindertransport. He wrote: "All those present joined in the song, and we forgot about the harsh world outside. Naturally, as on all such occasions, this was followed with festive food and drink. We all went home with hope in our hearts."

Books take on a form or shape of their own; this one has come together a bit like the concert Freddie described, or perhaps simply like a group of people gathered together to tell their stories. We'll primarily follow the lives of three people: Professor Leslie Baruch Brent, Ruth Oppenheimer David, and Marianne Josephy Elsley. You might think of them as soloists. Added to their experiences is a chorus of others who chime in, sometimes alone and other times as part of the Voices sections. There are, of course, thousands of stories like those told here, and I encourage you to explore books listed in the bibliography as well as websites provided in the resources section.

Learning about the resilience and courage of these children, parents, and rescuers has been humbling. I am only able to share these stories thanks to the generosity of Kindertransport survivors and their families. I am also indebted to those museums and organizations dedicated to preserving the testimonies of those who have borne witness to the Holocaust. We may think that the atrocities of the Holocaust are part of the distant past. But it was not so long ago. And there are still people who commit hate crimes, treat refugees harshly, and speak and act violently against others. I am writing these words in October 2018, a day after the worst anti-Semitic violence in United States history, when eleven people were killed at the Tree of Life Synagogue in Pittsburgh, Pennsylvania.

I once had the chance to meet Niels Skov, a resistance fighter in World War II, who helped rescue Jewish families in Denmark who were about to be deported by the Germans. He wasn't part of an organized group. He and a friend, like thousands of other Danes, simply found their own way to help and take action to do what was right. Niels has since passed away. He was ninety-four when we met. When I asked what advice he would give to young people today, Niels said, "Swim against the stream. Don't do what everyone else does."

I think it's up to each of us to take a stand against anti-Semitism, genocide, and discrimination, and to commit ourselves to justice, fairness, and kindness. We may not be able to change the entire world. But what we do matters. We can be brave and raise our voices to make sure others are not silenced, hurt, or bullied.

Think of them.

Here are the main voices in this book. A list of other Kindertransport survivors, as well as rescuers and historians, can be found in About the People in This Book (page 259).

A circular label removed from the suitcase used by Margot Stern when she was sent on a Kindertransport to England in December 1938.

PROFESSOR LESLIE BARUCH BRENT is a distinguished immunologist and the author of *Sunday's Child? A Memoir.* He was born in Germany in 1925 and escaped in December 1938 on the first Kindertransport. He lives in London. In November 2018 he spoke at the eightieth reunion of the Kindertransport.

RUTH OPPENHEIMER DAVID was born in Frankfurt, Germany, on March 17, 1929, and grew up in a small town. She escaped on the Kindertransport in June 1939. A retired teacher and author of a memoir entitled *Child of Our Time: A Young Girl's Flight from the Holocaust*, Ruth lives in Leicester, England, where she still speaks about her experience as a refugee.

MARIANNE JOSEPHY ELSLEY was born in Rostock, Germany, in 1923. An only child, she was fifteen when she left Germany in January 1939. She died in 2009. Quotations from her unpublished memoir, "Without Bitterness," are included here by permission of the Leo Baeck Institute and her daughter, Judith Elsley. Marianne also published a memoir, *A Chance in Six Million.*

CONTENTS

Part One

WHEN THEY BURN BOOKS

1925–1938

*Dort wo man Bücher verbrennt,
verbrennt man auch am Ende
Menschen.*
(Where they burn books, they will,
in the end, burn human beings too.)

—HEINRICH HEINE, *ALMANSOR*, 1823

Crisis was Hitler's oxygen.
He needed it to survive.

—IAN KERSHAW

When the Nazis proclaimed their
war against the Jewish people,
beginning with the boycott of April
1, 1933, the German Jews began to
understand the writing on the wall,
to realize that the foundations of
their life were tottering, and that
they must prepare themselves and
their children for a new and hard
struggle in a changed world.

—NORMAN BENTWICH

Nazi book burning in Berlin,
May 10, 1933.

A family picnic in pre-Nazi Germany. The young woman pictured is the mother of Kindertransport survivor Ruth David. Ruth's maternal grandfather is on the right, and her grandmother, Feodora, is on the far left. Ruth's youngest sister was named Feo after this grandmother.

Chapter One

BEFORE

B efore they were refugees, before they were victims, before they were survivors, they were ordinary children and teens. They were like you.

These children lived in small towns and big cities. They went to school and did homework. Their parents were shop owners, salespeople, lawyers, nurses, doctors, and teachers. They had brothers and sisters, grandparents, aunts and uncles, cousins, schoolmates, friends.

These children came from a variety of religious backgrounds. Some lived in traditional Orthodox Jewish families, where Judaism was an integral part of daily life. Their families followed Jewish customs and laws governing food and not working on Saturday, the Sabbath.

Some children were half Jewish, with one Jewish parent. Others lived in families that celebrated major Jewish religious holidays but also took part in secular, or nonreligious, aspects of holidays like Christmas and Easter. For instance, they might have a Christmas tree or hunt for Easter eggs, but not go to a Christian church. And there were some children who had one or more grandparents who were Jewish but didn't identify closely with being Jewish, or with any religion. Religion simply wasn't a large part of their lives.

No matter what their background, these children definitely liked to have fun. They didn't have computers or televisions when they were young, but they loved to ice-skate, ride bikes, play ball, and read books. These children, just like you, had dreams of their own. They hoped to grow up, travel, go to college, find work, or perhaps have a family someday.

And then their world turned upside down. Nothing was the same as it had been before.

Before.

Leslie
SUMMERS BY THE SEA

Books take years to research, write, revise, edit, and print. During the time I've been working on this one, I've had the privilege of getting to know (mostly through email and phone) several of the people whose stories you will read about here. One is Professor Leslie Baruch Brent, a Kindertransport refugee who grew up to become a renowned scientist.

In the summer of 2018, I sent Professor Brent another book I wrote about World War II. (He kindly said I could call him Leslie, so I will.) Leslie emailed to say he had read it while spending time with his wife, Carol, at a cottage in Brittany, France. I'm not sure if Leslie stayed near the sea, but I wonder if this vacation reminded him of summers long ago, when he was a boy in Germany.

Leslie Brent was born Lothar (Lo-tar) Baruch in Köslin, Germany, a northern town by the Baltic Sea that is now Koszalin, Poland. Later, after he moved to England, Leslie decided at age eighteen to volunteer for the British army. It was still wartime and, as Leslie explained, he wanted "to serve my newly adopted country and to help in the liberation of my family. I was not to know until years later that by the time I enlisted they were already dead." In the army, he was required to change his name in case he was captured by the Germans. Leslie decided to keep the same initials; he chose Brent as his last name and took his new first name from a popular British actor of the time named Leslie Howard.

Leslie Brent's birth year, 1925, is an important one in German history, and a good place to start our Kindertransport story. In March of that year, a German war hero named Paul von Hindenburg was elected for a seven-year term as president of Germany's Weimar Republic. The Weimar Republic was the new democratic government set up in Germany at the end of World War I; Hindenburg was its second president.

That same year also saw the publication of the first volume of *Mein Kampf*, a book by a thirty-six-year-old World War I veteran from Austria named Adolf Hitler. In 1921, Hitler had become chairman of the National Socialist German Workers' Party, also known as the Nazi Party. He riled up audiences, exploiting people's fear and anger, and blaming all of Germany's problems on Jews. Early on, Hitler created a personal protection guard, an army of storm troopers called the Sturmabteilung, or SA. Their nickname was "brownshirts," because of the color of their uniforms. Jewish children like those whose stories are in this book soon got used to seeing the brownshirts on the streets and came to fear them.

$\sim$

Leslie Brent was still a young boy during the years Hitler was consolidating his power. Leslie and his family lived peacefully in their small town of Köslin, far from the center of politics.

Leslie's father was a traveling salesman, and one of Leslie's earliest memories was meeting his father when he returned from a work trip. "Carrying in each hand a heavy suitcase containing not only his clothes but also his many samples, he was invariably the first to emerge from the platform and was proudly escorted home by me."

When home, the family enjoyed Sunday-afternoon walks in the nearby forest with close friends. Afterward, while the adults relaxed at a café, Leslie and his older sister, Eva Susanne, liked to roam through the woods. They tried not to get their toy planes stuck in the branches of trees. The children also learned to whistle the bars of a song to let the adults know where they were. Leslie never forgot that family whistle and later taught it to his children.

Va, as Leslie called his father, loved music and sang in a men's choir; he was fond of composing poems for special occasions.

"He had been a soldier during the First World War and had served as a medical orderly. Having rescued an injured soldier under fire he was awarded the Iron Cross," Leslie wrote of his father. "I am pretty certain that he later felt this would afford him some protection during the Nazi regime. It must have added to his false sense of security, and it certainly failed to save him and his family, in common with many others who had served their country during that war."

Leslie's older sister, Eva, was a skilled pianist. "To this day I have feelings of guilt towards her . . . on a sweltering summer's day I stole ten pennies from her purse so that I could buy myself an ice cream. I must have been six or seven at the time."

Leslie remembers a childhood full of make-believe games, spinning wooden tops, and reading adventure stories. On the way to school on a Monday morning, he liked to stop at the confectioner's shop and for ten pennies get a small bag of leftover cakes and candies.

"We made our own yoghurt by leaving bowls of unpasteurized milk in the open until it set and a skin formed—delicious with sugar, or when available, bilberries [a European berry related to blueberries] that we had picked in the woods. In the winter we baked apples on the shelf of our tiled oven, which also provided the flat [apartment] with heat."

For a summer vacation, Leslie's parents rented a small seaside cottage from a farmer. Since Köslin was only about seven miles from the Baltic Sea, they could travel to the shore by train. At that time, many of the farmhouses had thatched roofs. As the train chugged along, Leslie liked to count the stork nests in the chimneys.

At the beach, Leslie ran across the hot sand to keep his feet from blistering. He built sandcastles and swam, using the closest sandbank from shore as a landmark. He watched in awe as his father ventured far out into the water, swimming to the third sandbank.

"It was indeed a simple and innocent life."

Marianne
COLD BLUEBERRY SOUP

Marianne Josephy Elsley loved summers too. Marianne was born on June 23, 1923, in the town of Rostock, Germany. She passed away in 2009, but I've been in touch with her daughter, Judy, who helps to keep her mother's story alive. Marianne self-published a book about her life, entitled *A Chance in Six Million*; she also donated a memoir she wrote, "Without Bitterness," to the Leo Baeck Institute to help others understand the Holocaust. Marianne's home of Rostock, like Leslie Brent's town, is located north of Berlin, near the Baltic Sea. Today, their birthplaces are only about a five-hour car ride apart.

Marianne was an only child, but she had wonderful memories of her extended family. Summers were the time when her grandmother Josephy made her delicious fruit soups. "These were eaten cold and made of red currants, blackberries, or, most prized of all, local blueberries picked by us in the nearby forest or bought in the market," Marianne remembered. Since such dark, rich fruit could stain the tablecloth, these summer treats were ladled out and eaten very carefully.

Grandmother Josephy was a dignified, imposing matriarch. Each week, she hosted a family gathering, serving a delicious Sunday dinner. Sometimes there was even homemade ice cream, "a crunchy, creamy chocolate mixture." This was indeed a special treat, Marianne recalled, because although in those days you could buy ice cream at some restaurants, not everyone had refrigerators, so ice cream wasn't available in stores the way it is now.

Grandmother Josephy's well-stocked, grand kitchen was a wonder to a young child. "I remember being allowed to inspect her storeroom and larders with her, and being surprised at the quantities of eggs, hams, sausages and all sorts of things to which we did not aspire at home," Marianne said. "My father, her youngest son, always claimed that he could manage to survive on potatoes for the week as long as he had that Sunday meal, and he looked forward to it. I have mental glimpses of the splendid dining room, my uncles, aunts and cousins seated round an enormous table."

Marianne would have to hold on to that picture for the rest of her life. It would be all she had. Her family, like millions of others, would be broken apart forever.

Ruth
FAIRY-TALE FORESTS

Ruth Oppenheimer David grew up in the village of Fränkisch-Crumbach, in the Odenwald region of southwest Germany. Ruth was born in 1929. When she was young, not many people in her town owned cars; farmers used ox-drawn wagons for farmwork, or drove a horse and cart. Her picturesque village boasted red-roofed houses with gardens and an array of small shops. It was an easy walk to meadows full of flowers, hills, orchards, and the woods, which were rich in legends.

"The Odenwald forests for me were closely interwoven with the fairy tales of the brothers Grimm," remembered Ruth. "I even thought I knew where Little Red Riding Hood may have met her wolf and where the Sleeping Beauty might be hidden. I would not have been surprised to have encountered the Hansel and Gretel gingerbread house on one of our walks through the dense, scented, silent dark green woods."

Although there were few Jewish families in town,

Ruth and her family felt comfortable in their community. Her grandfather had grown up there, and *his* grandfather had arrived years before. "I knew that my family was Jewish but did not at the time understand how this made us different from other people. We were part of the village. As children we played with the village children."

Ruth's father, Moritz Oppenheimer, was a successful businessman who ran a cigar factory. His first wife

Ruth David's mother holds Ruth's older sister Hannah, born in 1926.

died, leaving him with three young children; the eldest was Anni, and there were also two boys, Ernst and Werner. His second wife, Grete, Ruth's mother, was from the city of Frankfurt, where she'd studied mathematics at the university. Ruth was never sure how her parents met, but she thought the move must have been a big change for her mother. After all, she'd been able to attend opera and theater performances in Frankfurt. Her husband's village didn't even have a library.

Ruth's mother also had to adjust to caring for three motherless children. Anni became ill with tuberculosis and, despite the family's efforts, later died. Ruth looked up to her older half brothers, Ernst and Werner. Ruth's mother and father added to the family and had

Hannah and baby Ruth.

four children together. First there was Hannah, then Ruth, and Michael. The baby of the family was Ruth's little sister, Feo, who was born in 1934 and named for their grandmother Feodora.

Baby Feo brought laughter and fun into the family. Ruth recalled Feo following her older siblings everywhere and cheerfully taking part in games like hide-and-seek. But Feo usually spoiled the surprise: "She always joyfully revealed hiding places by squealing in her puppy-dog way."

Although Michael and Feo Oppenheimer could not know it then, their lives would depend on their ability to stay hidden.

Hannah and her grandmother Feodora's dog.

While I haven't met Ruth David in person, I almost feel as if I know her. When I discovered her wonderful book, *Child of Our Time: A Young Girl's Flight from the Holocaust,* I learned she'd volunteered with the National Holocaust Centre and Museum in London; the staff there kindly connected us. I love when I wake up to find a delightful email message from her. She lives in Leicester, England, eight hours ahead of my home in Oregon. She keeps in touch with her sister Feo, who lives in Paris. The two sisters speak in French together. On Ruth's ninetieth birthday, on March 17, 2019, Feo and Michael traveled from France to celebrate with their older sister. What a wonderful reunion!

At ninety, Ruth still uses her voice to speak out to help others. Recently she spoke at an event in Leicester about the plight of Syrian refugees. Several years ago, Ruth received Germany's prestigious Order of Merit award recognizing her efforts visiting German schools and talking to young people about her family's experiences during the Holocaust. As you read here about her life as a girl in Nazi Germany, you might want to "meet" her too by following the link below.

LOOK, LISTEN, REMEMBER: You can listen to Ruth David speak about her life in a September 18, 2012, BBC News interview. To find it, use these search terms: Leicester Woman Honoured by Germany for Holocaust Work BBC. (Please note the British spell *honor* with a *u*—honour.) The URL address is: https://www.bbc.com/news/av/uk-england-leicestershire-19641062/leicester-woman-honoured-by-germany-for-holocaust-work.

JUDAISM

Judaism is a religion that dates back to the ancient Hebrews, who lived thousands of years ago. Jews were the first to believe in one God, and they follow the practices, laws, and traditions written in the Torah, the first five books of the Hebrew Bible. Jews believe God dictated the Torah to the prophet Moses on Mount Sinai after their exodus from slavery in Egypt. The Torah contains commandments that guide Jewish life.

Like all religions, Judaism has special holidays and traditions. Shabbat, or Sabbath, is a day of rest observed each week. Shabbat begins at sundown on Friday and ends at nightfall Saturday. There are prayer services, songs, and special meals and blessings, and many Jewish families attend services at a synagogue.

Another important holiday is Passover, which commemorates the liberation of the Israelite slaves from Egypt. It is marked by services and eating unleavened food for a week. Rosh Hashanah is the Jewish New Year; Yom Kippur, or the Day of Atonement, is the holiest day of the year. Hanukkah, celebrated every winter, is an eight-day festival of lights commemorating the ancient Jews' miraculous victory over the mighty Seleucid Empire that was oppressing them.

Today, there are fewer than fifteen million Jews in the world. Although they are a small minority,

comprising less than 0.2 percent of the overall population, Jews have been persecuted throughout history.
Christianity has had a long and complicated relationship with Judaism. Throughout the centuries, many
people wrongly accused Jews of killing Jesus Christ, and
many more argued that Jesus's teachings make Judaism
obsolete. As a result, malicious conspiracy theories have
been spread to malign Jewish people. Through the ages,
Jews have been forced to convert. Many more have been
discriminated against, expelled, or even murdered. Only
in 1879, however, was a word finally coined to describe
this hatred of Jews: *anti-Semitism*.

In many ways, the anti-Semitism promoted by the
Nazis had a lot in common with the ancient, religious-
based kind. But Hitler and his followers advanced
poisonous new theories and ideas. They argued that
Jews were subhuman, while people of Aryan, or Nordic,
heritage were superior. Even though Jews had lived
peacefully in Germany for generations and had become
prominent leaders in the arts, industry, and academia,
the Nazis used pseudoscience to claim that Jews were
inferior. At the same time, Nazi newspapers, radio
broadcasts, and films argued that the nation's Jews
were conspiring against their non-Jewish neighbors
and were behind all of Germany's troubles, from war to
economic hardships.

To address what they called "the Jewish problem,"

the Nazis passed laws that made Jewish lives progressively more difficult. Jews were initially forbidden from attending most schools, working in most professions, or owning property. They were later deported to crowded ghettos, where many died of illness or hunger, and later still to concentration or death camps, resulting in the murder of six million Jewish men, women, and children.

The Catholic Church officially declared in 1965 that neither the Jews of Jesus's time nor their descendants were responsible for the death of Christ—a belief strongly shared by nearly all churches today. Nevertheless, like other kinds of racism and religious discrimination, anti-Semitism still exists. Some people continue to spread ancient conspiracy theories about the Jews. Others even claim, against overwhelming historical evidence, that the Holocaust never happened.

According to the Federal Bureau of Investigation, in 2018, anti-Semitic attacks soared to the highest level in two decades. If you see or hear anti-Semitic comments or are a target yourself, please find a trusted adult to tell. Look for a helper who can guide you in finding ways to respond safely.

LOOK, LISTEN, REMEMBER: If you are not Jewish yourself, you can learn more about Judaism by reading or asking questions of a Jewish friend. The United States Holocaust Memorial Museum (USHMM) has a learning site for students here: https://encyclopedia.ushmm.org/content/en /project/the-holocaust-a-learning-site-for-students. The Anti-Defamation League (ADL), an organization established to protect the Jewish people and secure justice and fair treatment for all, provides resources to help prevent bullying and promote ally behavior. Find out more about ADL at: https:// www.adl.org/education-and-resources /resources-for-educators-parents-families.

Voices

LIFE BEFORE THE NAZIS

Ruth David didn't share memories from her life for a long time. Her children encouraged her to write her story, but, she said, she always found some excuse to delay revisiting a painful past. She told her daughter, "I shall start when I have learnt how to use the computer."

Eventually, Ruth did agree to write her memoir. In the same way, Lisa Leist Seiden was moved to write her story so her grandchildren could learn more about their family history. But it was for herself too. "Oh, those memories . . . ," she wrote. "They are like naughty gnomes. They play with us. They appear without asking. At other times they hide or fade away. . . . Some make us happy, others sad, they turn us round and round."

Lisa realized it was important to find a way to live with these memories.

The three sisters pictured here (all part of the Anker family) lived in Berlin before World War II and later escaped on a Kindertransport.

WINTER WONDERS

Lisa's memories of her childhood help us imagine her life in a quiet suburb of Vienna, Austria, where she was born in 1929. Austria shared a border with its more powerful neighbor, Germany. In 1938, Austria was occupied by the Nazis, which immediately resulted in anti-Semitic restrictions and persecutions.

But before that, Lisa's childhood was filled with wonder. Her mother loved reading, playing the piano, and going to the opera. Her father had fought in World War I. He had come from a poor family but had worked and studied hard to become a chemical engineer.

Lucie Eisenstab Porges rides her tricycle in a park in Vienna, around 1930. Her family left Austria in 1938 and eventually escaped to Switzerland. Her future husband, Paul, also from Vienna, escaped on a Kindertransport.

One of Lisa's favorite toys was her dollhouse, which had little windows that could open and close, tiny furniture pieces, and movable dolls. Winters were cold; the lakes froze and snow sparkled. Lisa and her brother, Peter, liked to go sledding in the park, where she fed furry squirrels with chestnuts from her own hand. "Sometimes when passing under some pine branch, heavy and white, I would open my mouth wide and shaking the branch a bit, let some of the frosty snow fall into it. I thought it fun to listen to the crunchy sound it made between my teeth."

Lisa and Peter, who was five years older, also loved to ice-skate at a rink after school. Lisa enjoyed having a big brother who could teach her things like climbing trees. He was fun to go skating with too. "Sometimes he allowed me to hold onto the tail of his jacket and I would stop skating and let myself be pulled along while he picked up speed, body inclined, head forward, arms swinging. Round and round we'd go. Then, tired, our skates hanging from our necks, [we'd] walk home in the early winter dusk."

Inside, Lisa loved to look at the patterns that the frost made on the windowpanes. Nose pressed against the glass, she could imagine other worlds. "I could discover castles perched on the slopes of peaky mountains, tall trees and deep valleys and how this white labyrinth changed color when illuminated by the golden rays of

A young Jewish child, Berta Rosenheim Hertz, sits at a table full of toys on the terrace of her home in Leipzig, Germany, in 1929. Hertz later escaped on a Kindertransport.

the sun," she said. But Peter wasn't interested in this sort of thing. "When I called my brother to come and see what I saw, he would ask me to leave him alone and let him get on with his stamp collection."

EVERYTHING WAS HOMEMADE

Alfred "Freddie" Traum was also born in Vienna in 1929. He lived with his parents and older sister, Ruth. Judaism was important in his home, and one of his favorite memories was watching his mother cook for the Sabbath. Freddie savored the delectable aromas that filled the apartment. Even years later, catching a whiff of the same meals his mother had made could whisk him back in time.

"Preparing for the Sabbath actually began Thursdays, with my mother laying out large round thinly rolled dough that she would later use to make noodles for soup. She busied herself in the kitchen all evening making mouthwatering selections of cakes that would last through the entire week. We never bought any ready-made cakes. Everything was homemade."

Freddie was also close to his father, who'd become disabled serving in the Austrian army in World War I. He used two walking canes and spent a lot of time in their apartment. But Freddie's father was never idle and was especially gifted with his hands.

"Although he never trained to be a tailor, he handled the sewing machine like a professional, making all kinds of clothes for us and even a new suit for me," Freddie said. "He could turn his hands to all sorts of activities, resoling shoes, repairing electrical apparatuses [gadgets] that had ceased to function, and even tinkering with the radio when it went on the blink and somehow managing to get it functioning again.

"He was also an amateur photographer, doing his own developing and printing. We never went to a photography studio; as a result, I only have small snapshots, which he had made himself. As a little boy I used to watch his every move, picking up many cues that I would store away for use at some future day. He never complained about his handicap. I learned so much from him, but, above all, he taught me how to live with adversity and make the most of it."

F SHARP!

Hedi Stoehr (or Stöhr) Ballantyne lived in Vienna, Austria, where she was born on April 9, 1927. Her father, Richard Stoehr, was Jewish, but her mother was not. Hedi's father was a talented composer and music instructor who taught piano at the Academy of Music in Vienna, now called the University of Music and Performing Arts. The largest room of the family's apartment contained a grand piano; pictures of famous composers like Bach, Handel, and Mozart graced the walls.

Hedi was too intimidated to take lessons from her father. Instead, one of his students taught her. "One day when I was sitting at the piano practicing and he [her father] was sitting at his desk far away at the other end of the apartment he called out, 'F sharp, not F!' I was amazed that he could tell from far away what note I was supposed to play. I didn't know there was such a thing as perfect pitch. After that I always made sure that I did my practicing when he wasn't at home."

Composer and teacher Richard Stoehr in the family's Vienna apartment. This is the piano Hedi practiced on as a girl. Her father escaped to the United States, where he taught music at Saint Michael's College in Vermont. Hedi's mother remained in Germany; her brother went to Norway. Hedi escaped on a Kindertransport; after the war, the family was reunited in the United States.

Hedi slept on a couch in the piano salon that could be made into a bed. "We had no bathroom in the apartment but used the communal toilet in the hall. Instead of toilet paper we used newspaper torn into small sheets and hung on a nail. There was also a water faucet for cold water in the hallway," Hedi explained. "Each of the three families on that floor filled up their pitchers there. For baths the water was heated on the gas stove in the kitchen and poured into a zinc tub with a back to lean against."

For summer vacation, her parents left the city of Vienna behind and rented a room in an old farmhouse in the Austrian countryside. In addition to playing in the hay, Hedi loved helping the milkmaid's daughter lead the cows to and from the pasture.

"I would accompany her nearly every day and we played while we took care of the cows. There wasn't much to do unless flies bothered the cows and they started galloping through the fields of oats and rye which were planted on the steep slopes. . . . It was a challenge to calm them down and get them to go back to grazing. My mother had had a little hut built for us as a shelter and we played house, or cracked hazelnuts which we gathered in the hedges.

"Another of my favorite activities on the farm was to ride along on the hay wagon, pulled by oxen, when the farmer was haying [haymaking]. It was soft and tickly and wonderfully sweet smelling."

The farmers in the area were mostly Catholic, and Hedi sometimes enjoyed going to the lovely village church. She loved the smell of incense. When Hedi was nine, one of the local boys surprised her with a kiss while they were playing.

Hedi and her family felt safe on this farm in the countryside. But those wonderful summers would not last.

Chapter Two

HITLER'S RISE TO POWER

One day as she was walking home from school in the city, Hedi Ballantyne found herself on the edge of a large crowd gathered in a central plaza in Vienna. Curious, she stopped to listen. She realized the man speaking was Adolf Hitler.

"He shouted and raved, and the people around me were inflamed by his magnetic oratory. They were soon whipped into a kind of frenzy by him," Hedi remembered. "I was caught in the crowd, knowing that the hatred was directed at Jews, and that included me.

"It scared me terribly and yet I was fascinated. What caused the people to react in this way to the man with the little moustache?"

Hedi's question would puzzle many others—then and now. Just how did this obscure, strange misfit of a man rise to the position of power of a major European country? How did Adolf Hitler manage to convince so many to follow him and carry out his unthinkable atrocities against millions of innocent men, women, and children?

There are no simple answers. But, as Hitler's biographer Ian Kershaw has noted, "It can be said with certainty: without Hitler, history would have been different."

Adolf Hitler was born on April 20, 1889, into a middle-class family in Austria. From all accounts, he genuinely loved his mother, though he had a difficult relationship with his stern, bad-tempered father. After high school, Hitler defied his father, who wanted him to take a civil service job in an office. Instead, Hitler applied to the Academy of Fine Arts in Vienna, with the vision of becoming a great artist. In late 1907, the school rejected him. Even so, following his mother's death around the same time, he moved to Vienna in February 1908.

Hitler drifted during the next five years. He liked to attend concerts but wanted to listen to only the grand German music of the past, especially the operas of composer Richard Wagner (1813–1883), who had

Hitler, flanked by the massed ranks of the Sturmabteilung (SA), ascends the steps to the speaker's podium during the 1934 harvest festival celebration. The festivals were a Nazi propaganda extravaganza.

achieved the status of a supreme artist. Hitler had those same ambitions. He didn't want to work at a regular job though. When his money ran out, Hitler painted postcard-size pictures to sell. Although it's not quite clear how it happened, many historians think that Hitler's time in Vienna marked the beginning of his anti-Semitic views—his hatred of Jews.

In 1913, Hitler moved to Munich, Germany. When World War I began, Hitler joined the army. Wounded in 1916, he returned to action but was sidelined in 1918 by an attack of mustard gas. Like many others, he felt devastated by Germany's defeat. Hitler turned to politics in 1919.

Hitler's speeches tapped into a national sense of anger, hatred, and resentment about Germany's loss in the war. Hitler condemned the harsh terms of the Treaty of Versailles in 1919, which held Germany responsible for the war and required it to pay steep reparations that drained the economy and made recovery difficult.

In September 1919, Hitler joined the German Workers' Party. In 1920, the group was renamed the Nationalsozialistische Deutsche Arbeiterpartei (NSDAP or Nazi Party). At a mass meeting in Munich on February 24, 1920, Hitler's speech electrified the audience. He made his listeners believe that only he could solve Germany's problems. He railed against England and France, claiming their goal was to entirely destroy Germany. He portrayed himself as strongly anti-Communist as well.

But the main theme running through each and every speech was Hitler's hatred of Jews, whom he blamed for everything. Historian Kershaw described Hitler's use of propaganda to make Jewish people the enemy. "Behind all evil that had befallen or was threatening Germany stood the figure of the Jew. In speech after speech he lashed the Jew in the most vicious and barbaric language imaginable."

Anti-Semitism had existed in Europe and Russia for a long time. Hitler's speeches fueled existing racist views and gave ordinary Germans someone to blame. Hitler's message appealed to people's most base and negative emotions. "His audiences loved it. More than anything else, these attacks evoked torrents of applause and cheering," explained Kershaw. "His technique— beginning slowly, plenty of sarcasm, personalized attacks on named targets, then a gradual crescendo to a climax—whipped his audiences into a frenzy."

Hitler became the face and voice of NSDAP, mobilizing crowds that gathered in Munich's large beer halls. In politics and speechmaking, Hitler had found his purpose: He became a drummer for his new national right-wing movement. In other words, he would help rally others to the cause.

To deal with packed events, Hitler started a protection unit in the mid-1920s. This group evolved into the Sturmabteilung, the assault division, or storm troopers. The brownshirts grew into a feared paramilitary organization that carried out acts of violence and intimidation throughout the country.

$\sim$

In November 1923, Hitler and the Nazi Party attempted to seize power in Munich. The failed coup, called the Beer Hall Putsch, was soon put down. Hitler was arrested and put on trial for treason. He was sentenced to five years in prison. The NSDAP was banned.

Hitler took away several important lessons from this experience: He realized that to be successful, his movement must get power not by revolution but by legal means. Not only that, he became convinced his true role was not as the drummer for his cause, but as its one and only leader.

While in prison, Hitler wrote the first volume of

Adolf Hitler leaving Landsberg prison on December 20, 1924, after serving just nine months for treason during the Beer Hall Putsch.

his autobiography, *Mein Kampf,* which means "My Struggle." (The second volume was published in December 1926.) In *Mein Kampf,* Hitler set out many of the extreme, racist positions he would make all too real in the years to come. These views included vicious anti-Semitic rhetoric attacking Jews as a "parasite" race and declaring Aryans as the master or "genius"

Adolf Hitler in 1933, the year he became chancellor of Germany.

race. The Nazis used the term *Aryan* to refer to non-Jewish Caucasians having Nordic features: white skin, blue eyes, and fair hair.

Hitler's trial for treason and prison sentence should have put a stop to his political ambitions. In fact, had he been punished for longer, the course of history might well have been different. Instead, Hitler was released for good behavior in about nine months. He was back on the political scene by early 1925, once again giving fiery speeches. The NSDAP was reestablished and began to gain supporters and momentum. Hitler continued to work at creating a cult, with him at the top, as the führer, or leader.

On October 24, 1929, the United States stock market crashed, ushering in the Great Depression. Negative effects were felt worldwide and were particularly devastating to Germany's fragile economy. In elections that fall, the Nazi Party had a surprisingly good showing. The next year, in September 1930, the Nazis moved from claiming twelve seats in the German parliament to holding more than a hundred, making it the second largest party. "Almost 6½ million Germans now voted for Hitler's party—eight times as many as two years earlier," wrote Kershaw. "The Nazi bandwagon was rolling."

Hitler proved adept at politics; the Nazis continued to gain power and influence in the months that followed. Then, on January 30, 1933, German president Paul von Hindenburg named Hitler to the post of chancellor. Hitler had gone from being an unknown to running one of the major countries of Europe—with no qualifications to manage a major government. He was now the führer, on his way to becoming the most despicable tyrant in history.

Hitler's position was strengthened in early March, when the Nazis won more than 40 percent of the vote and controlled 288 of the 647 seats in the new Reichstag, or parliament.

Throughout the country, Nazis quickly moved to take over local government operations. Through political maneuvering and the strong-arm tactics of his storm troopers, Hitler crushed opposition efforts. Within months, Hitler moved to dismantle the Weimar Republic and establish Nazi Germany, the Third Reich. *Reich* is a German word meaning "kingdom" or "empire." *Third Reich* was a Nazi propaganda term asserting that Nazi rule would be Germany's third realm, the successor to

On the day of his appointment as German chancellor, Adolf Hitler greets a crowd of enthusiastic Germans from a window in the Chancellery building. Berlin, Germany, January 30, 1933.

the Holy Roman Empire (800–1806) and the German Empire (1871–1918).

Germany was now in the hands of what historian Ian Kershaw has called "the dangerous leader of a political gangster-mob." The cult of the leader took hold throughout German society. German journalist Sebastian Haffner observed, "The whole tradition of a state based on the rule of law . . . which had seemed so firm and permanent, had disappeared overnight."

Jewish citizens had been watching Hitler's rise with apprehension. They hoped that, once in power, Hitler would drop his extreme views and govern in a responsible way. People depended on their nation's laws to protect them; they believed the institutions of society

Chancellor Adolf Hitler addresses the Reichstag, the German parliament.

would hold. After all, Jewish people held important positions in banks, hospitals, and universities throughout Germany. Jewish families thought they could rely on friends and neighbors. Many Jewish men had fought valiantly for their country in the First World War and remained proud and loyal patriots.

Yet almost immediately after Hitler became chancellor, Jews found themselves targeted by the new government. On April 1, there was a boycott of Jewish businesses. Other laws restricted Jewish lawyers and doctors. Jews were soon forced out of civil service positions, journalism, and the arts. Limits were placed on the number of Jewish children in public schools. There was little or no protest anywhere, even when new laws meant that prominent university professors (who held civil service positions) were fired and forced to leave the country.

While not everyone believed Hitler would follow through on his anti-Semitic rhetoric, one man was not fooled. Rabbi Leo Baeck was a scholar and the spiritual leader of the Jewish community in Germany. Soon after Hitler came to power he made a sober prediction: "'The end of German Jewry has arrived.'"

Historians estimate that in 1933 between five hundred thousand and six hundred thousand Jews lived in Germany. About one-third of the Jewish population was clustered in Berlin; many others lived in major cities like Frankfurt, Hamburg, and Cologne.

What should these thousands of families do? How should they cope with this kind of hate-filled speech? Should they stay, hoping that Hitler's hold on power would be over soon? Should they assume that things would get better? And if they decided to go, what country would have them? How could they just pick up and leave their homes, businesses, and communities?

These were the questions the children of the Kindertransport grew up hearing their parents argue and debate.

There were few good answers.

HITLER'S YOUNG NEIGHBOR

Edgar Feuchtwanger was born in Munich, Germany, in 1924. He was the nephew of Lion Feuchtwanger, a well-known Jewish novelist and outspoken critic of the Nazis and their leader.

Edgar grew up hearing the grown-ups around him debate politics—especially the political career of their neighbor Adolf Hitler, who lived in an apartment across the street. At first, some of Edgar's relatives thought there was no need to take Hitler very seriously. After all, it was hard to imagine him leading the nation. "'Hitler's a thug . . . a schemer leading a band of good-for-nothings,'" Edgar heard his uncle Lion say.

But Edgar's father had read Hitler's *Mein Kampf* and was convinced the Nazi leader was a dangerous maniac. Edgar agreed: He felt frightened just looking out his window at the crowds of storm troopers marching near Hitler's apartment.

"Waves of Nazis flowed between our house and Hitler's. They kept coming all day long. Hitler's SA

Hitler along with Hermann Göring and other Nazis saluting beneath a huge Nazi banner on the street during a procession in Munich, Germany.

marched in nice straight lines, like a real army, all wearing red armbands with a white circle and a swastika in the center. They held their arms outstretched toward their leader's room, calling his name, bellowing 'Heil Hitler! Heil Hitler!' and the windows reverberated like drums to this endless roar."

Once, Edgar ran into Hitler on the street. This took place in 1930, when he was about six years old and taking a walk with his nanny.

"He's right in front of us, outside his building. We've stopped in our tracks . . . I can see he's cut himself shaving, as my father sometimes does. He has blue eyes. I didn't know that. You can't see that in photos. I thought his eyes were completely black. I've never seen him so close up. He has hairs in his nose, and a few in his ears. He's shorter than I thought. . . .

"He looks at me. I should look away. But I can't. I stare at him. Maybe I should smile? I'm his neighbor, after all! Does he recognize me? Does he know I watch him from my bedroom? Can he see inside our house? . . . Does he know I'm Jewish? . . .

"I don't want him to hate me. Or my father. Or my mother. . . . He's climbed into a dark car, black as night, its lines as hard as stone."

Hitler did hate Jewish people like Edgar and his parents. Edgar began to hear his parents talking about whether they should try to leave Germany, as his uncle Lion was forced to do in 1933.

"'But where would we go? Who would have us?'" his father wondered. "'We'd need a work visa for whichever country we choose. We really can't settle illegally wherever takes our fancy. With this financial crash, foreigners everywhere are being accused of taking other people's jobs. . . .'"

LOOK, LISTEN, REMEMBER: Listen to Edgar Feuchtwanger talk about growing up across the street from Adolf Hitler: https://www.youtube.com /watch?v=9GX2OgRzNQ8. You can read more about Edgar's life here: https://www.bbc.co.uk/news /magazine-20210025.

Chapter Three

THE WORRYING TIME BEGINS

Ruth

MEN IN BROWN UNIFORMS

In Ruth David's village of Fränkisch-Crumbach, things began to change soon after Hitler became chancellor in 1933. Ruth noticed Hitler's picture displayed everywhere. And then there were the brownshirts, the storm troopers of the SA.

"Gradually more and more men appeared in brown uniforms," Ruth said. "They walked stiffly and threw out their arms in the 'Heil Hitler' greeting, which they made to sound like a hostile bark.

"Soldiers with rifles, or with spades over their shoulders, marched to military music through the village, singing Nazi songs which were meant to frighten us with threats of 'Jewish blood dropping from our knives' and proud declarations: *'Heute gehort uns Deutschland, morgen die ganze Welt'* ('Today Germany, tomorrow the whole world')."

The world Ruth's parents and grandparents had known was disappearing. "My grandmother had belonged to a society in which Jews were integrated and unafraid. They felt they belonged to a cultured, civilized nation, and were proud to be part of it."

Ruth's parents tried to shield her from outside events. But Ruth couldn't ignore what she saw with her own eyes. Nazi swastikas appeared on the armbands of soldiers, on postage stamps, and especially on flags. The flags seemed to be everywhere.

"Those monstrous, threatening flags. Blood-red around a white circle on which the menacing, angular black swastika seemed to spin. Every house had to sport one," Ruth recalled. "Not ours. As Jews we were forbidden such display, and the lack of flags helped to mark us. We became daily more estranged from the society we had always assumed was ours."

Other children sometimes put the hateful things they heard and saw into action. And to add to Ruth's fear, a girl in the village threatened to set a bulldog on her just because she was Jewish. "I was afraid of dogs and terrified." Walking to school became an ordeal.

Nazi propaganda was everywhere. Here, children's toys, including tin Nazi storm troopers and a toy ship with a Nazi sail, are displayed before a Christmas tree.

Marianne
AS LONG AS THEY ONLY SING

Marianne Elsley enjoyed school. She had fond memories of her first day, which was always celebrated as a special occasion. "On this day, German mothers meet their young from school armed with huge, conical, colored bags [or cardboard cones]. These contain sweets, fruit and other small presents, rather like the English Christmas stocking... I remember mine now—it was covered in brightly patterned orange paper, and among other things there was a tangerine in it," Marianne said.

Tangerines were exotic treats not usually sold in village shops at the time, making the gift even more memorable. Today, families still follow the tradition of school cones (Schultüte).

Portrait of Siegbert Fischer on his first day of school, holding the traditional Schultüte filled with candies. In July 1939, Siegbert and his sister were among the children who escaped the Nazis on a Kindertransport.

But then one day Marianne was called into the headmistress's office: Her parents had arrived to bring her home. Marianne was an only child, and her parents didn't want her walking home alone. The reason? A sign had been posted outside their house proclaiming them Jews, and there were men in brown uniforms and tall jackboots parading back and forth on the street in front of their home.

That incident marked the beginning. Bullying, teasing, and anti-Semitic barbs soon followed. "One walked in constant fear," Marianne said. "One went about trying to be inconspicuous, mingling with the crowds, never drawing attention to oneself, looking down at the pavement and never staring at someone. We were all very frightened."

Marianne's friends started to treat her differently. "The security of my own small world gradually began to give way. I remember my sorrow when I was not invited to the usual round of birthday parties. I was the only Jewish girl in my form [grade level] and I found to my shame and discomfort that my former friends would

Girls wait for the führer along a parade route. Millions of young Germans joined the Hitler Youth.

no longer sit next to me. . . . In the playground they were not allowed to talk to me or play with me. I walked around on my own."

It was much the same for her parents. It had become dangerous for other town residents to be associated with Jewish people. "They were simply not allowed to [talk to us], and risked their jobs and the goodwill of the authorities if they ignored these instructions," said Marianne. "I remember one very good friend who deliberately came across the street to greet my mother and speak to her. My mother was quite shocked and afraid for her [friend's] safety."

That woman's defiance was the exception. Most people seemed perfectly glad to turn their backs—or worse. "I remember one occasion, fairly early on, when there was a Sunday of harassment. Young men in brown uniforms were driven round the town in open lorries [trucks]. They stopped outside the houses where Jews were known to live and bawled obscene anti-Semitic songs. I was very frightened and blocked up my ears. My mother, white as a sheet, said comfortingly, 'As long as they only sing, it will be all right.'"

Marianne realized that the "innocent, calm, comfortable days were over—forever." Instead, "a worrying time started."

Leslie

WHEN JEWISH BLOOD SPURTS

Change came to the town of Köslin too, where Leslie Brent lived. Both his grandfather and uncle owned shops that lost customers; his father struggled to keep his sales job. Leslie's family was forced to move to a smaller apartment to save money.

"Non-Jewish Germans who had been friends, or at the very least had been friendly, began to melt away," Leslie recalled. His father had always politely lifted his hat and said a pleasant hello when passing neighbors in the street. Now people were greeting one another with a Hitler salute, throwing their hands into the air and shouting, *"Heil Hitler!"* meaning "Hail Hitler." Another greeting was *"Sieg Heil!,"* or "Hail victory."

One evening, Leslie and his sister witnessed a group of storm troopers marching and singing in the street. Each man held a flaming torch. "Eva and I watched behind the closed curtains with a strange mixture of fear and fascination. This incident made an indelible impression on me, and I remember the tune as well as the words only too well."

Translated, the song went like this: "'And when Jewish blood spurts from the knife then all is really well.'"

Brownshirts marching, sometime between 1936–1938.

Chapter Four

WHEN THEY BURN BOOKS

CAN'T YOU REPLACE HER?

Edith Rosenthal Lavender wasn't on a Kindertransport train, but her story helps us understand one of the important events that took place in Nazi Germany in the spring of 1933. Edith was born on November 24, 1913, in Wiesbaden, Germany. She was nineteen and working at her first job when the Nazis came to power. Edith loved playing the piano and enjoyed learning languages.

"We started French in the second grade, we started English in the fourth or fifth grade, and I took Spanish two years before I graduated. By the time I was through, when I was sixteen, because I started school when I was five, I was very fluent in three languages plus German."

Edith's language skills helped her land a job as a typist with I.G. Farben, a large German chemical company. Edith had already noticed that girls she'd gone to school with pretended not to know her anymore. A friend of her brother's once spat at her and called her names.

Her father lost his hardware shop around this time. "There was nobody to come in and buy," said Edith. "You can't keep a store going and pay the rent if you have nobody who buys. They [Nazis] were walking back and forth, [with a] big sign, *Kauft nicht bei Juden* ['Don't buy from Jews']. Who goes in there? Very few people have the courage to do that."

Then the harassment started at work. Someone wrote a letter to Edith's boss saying: "'Can't you replace the Jewess Edith Rosenthal with an Aryan girl?'"

At first, Edith received support from her supervisor, who replied, "'Yes, as soon as you get me someone who can take shorthand in English, French, and Spanish, I'll replace Fräulein [Miss] Rosenthal.'"

Yet the attacks from her coworkers only got worse. The other women were mean-spirited and hateful. "I was sitting in a place with maybe four other typists, when I had to type. I typed out everything. I was a very good typist, which probably had to do with my piano lessons," said Edith. "One day I put my work on one side and I went to lunch. When I came back, they had poured ink all over it."

German students gather around books they regard as "un-German." The books were publicly burned in Berlin on May 10, 1933.

One day in the spring of 1933, Edith received a call from the man who owned the local bookshop. He also operated a small lending library from his store. Edith loved to read and had become one of Mr. Schwab's regular customers.

"He called me and said, 'Fräulein Rosenthal, do you want to come tonight after dark? I put a box of books away for you. Do you want to have them? They're books by Jewish authors. Tomorrow I have to give all my books to the committee, and they're going to burn them.'"

Edith didn't hesitate. "So I went that night and got the books . . . I still have them."

BOOKS SAVED AND BOOKS LOST

The bookshop owner who set aside the box for Edith wasn't alone in wanting to save knowledge. In 1933, in Hamburg, Germany, a man named Fritz Saxl began to worry. Saxl was the director of the Warburg Library, a priceless collection of thousands of books compiled by the Jewish historian Aby Warburg. Could the library be preserved, or would the Nazis come for it?

Saxl and others wanted to make sure future generations could benefit from the library. With support from Warburg's brothers in the United States and a donor in England, the Warburg collection was moved to London in 1934. Today, its more than 350,000 volumes are part of the Warburg Institute at the University of London.

But most books—and readers—weren't so lucky. Book burnings took place in several cities in Germany in the spring of 1933. On the evening of May 10, approximately twenty thousand books were destroyed in an enormous bonfire in a large public square in Berlin. Some were written by modern German authors and Jewish writers of the past. Works by foreign authors

A member of the SA throws confiscated books into the bonfire during the public burning of "un-German" books on the Opernplatz (an open public square) in Berlin on May 10, 1933.

A public burning of books on the Opernplatz in Berlin.

such as Jack London, H. G. Wells, and Helen Keller were also destroyed.

Erich Kästner was the author of the popular German children's book *Emil and the Detectives* (1929). He attended the Berlin book burning but fled when someone recognized him and called out, "'There's Kästner!'"

That night, Hitler's new minister of propaganda, Dr. Joseph Goebbels, gave a speech as the flames reached to the sky. "'The soul of the German people can again express itself. These flames not only illuminate the final end of an old era; they also light up the new.'"

When newspapers in other countries reported on the book burnings, people spoke out to condemn these acts. One influential voice was the American activist

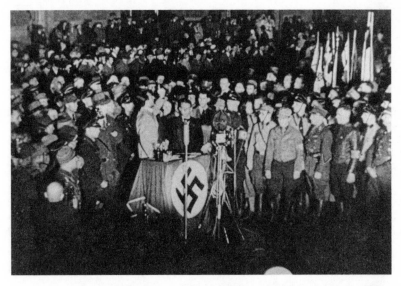

Propaganda minister Joseph Goebbels delivers a speech during the book burning on the Opernplatz on May 10, 1933.

and author Helen Keller, who'd lost her sight and hearing as a young child. She wrote an open letter to the university students of Germany participating in the destruction, which was published in the *New York Times*.

Helen Keller said, in part: "'History has taught you nothing if you think you can kill ideas. Tyrants have tried to do that often before, and the ideas have risen up in their might and destroyed them. You can burn my books and the books of the best minds in Europe, but the ideas in them have seeped through a million channels and will continue to quicken other minds.'"

Jewish writers such as Lion Feuchtwanger, uncle of Hitler's young neighbor Edgar, were key targets of the

Nazi book burning in Berlin. But Lion Feuchtwanger wasn't in Germany to witness it. On January 30, 1933, the day Hitler became chancellor, he happened to be on a book tour in the United States and was guest of honor at a dinner in Washington, DC, hosted by the German ambassador to the United States.

The next day, in a rare protest against the Nazis, the German ambassador resigned. The ambassador also called Lion Feuchtwanger with a warning: Don't go home. The author took that advice and instead went to France with his wife.

Jewish author Lion Feuchtwanger, uncle of Edgar, aboard the ship *Excalibur* after escaping the Nazis, in October 1940.

Later, he was put in an internment camp in France and very nearly deported to a concentration camp. Thanks to his wife's ingenuity, he made a daring escape in 1940. At one point, the author donned a shawl and dark glasses and pretended to be the mother-in-law of the American deputy consul. The couple settled in California. Today, Lion Feuchtwanger's collection of rare books and manuscripts form the Feuchtwanger Memorial Library at the University of Southern California.

HILLS OF BOOKS IN THE STREET

Growing up across the street from Hitler, young Edgar Feuchtwanger understood that his uncle's ideas and outspoken criticism of the Nazis made him dangerous to a regime intent on forcing everyone to think alike.

"Uncle Lion won't ever return to Germany. Hitler has stripped him of his nationality. All his books have been burned. Soldiers went into bookshops, confiscated them, then piled them in the street, so many of them they looked like hills. The soldiers doused them with gas and set them alight."

"Readers . . . were deprived of their world overnight," wrote Sebastian Haffner, a young German journalist living in Berlin at this time. Haffner wasn't Jewish, but he found the book burnings alarming. They were meant to scare ordinary German citizens—and they did. Haffner said that even when they were at home, people "felt intimidated and pushed their copies of Heinrich Mann and [Lion] Feuchtwanger into the back rows of their bookshelves." If friends wanted to discuss books in public, they did so in whispers.

Haffner also saw how the Nazis were trying to silence journalists like him. Haffner knew one newspaper editor who wrote something negative about the Nazis. That man lost his job and very nearly his life. It was clear the Nazis understood the power of a free press—and were determined to stifle and co-opt dissenting voices. "Many journals and newspapers disappeared from the kiosks—but what happened to those that continued in circulation was much more disturbing. You could not quite recognize them anymore.

"In a way a newspaper is like an old acquaintance: you instinctively know how it will react to certain events, what it will say about them and how it will express its views. If it suddenly says the opposite of what it said yesterday, denies its own past, distorting its features, you cannot avoid feeling that you are in a madhouse. That happened," Haffner said.

"Later, one became accustomed to this and picked up occasional hints by reading between the lines of articles on the arts pages. The political pages always kept strictly to the party line."

All this was part of the Nazification of culture and

society. The Nazis were set on controlling all aspects of life and thought: not just politics and policies but art, theater, journalism, and education too.

Since German professors were public, civil service employees, they could be fired by the government. It's estimated that a quarter of all professors were dismissed in the 1930s. Many Jewish intellectuals and scientists, including Nobel Prize–winning physicist Albert Einstein, fled to accept teaching and research jobs elsewhere, including the United States. At home, Einstein was called a villain, and new college courses in "racial sciences," exalting Nazi theories, were added to the curriculum.

Few faculty members at German universities mounted much of a protest to the book burnings, the rejection of scientific thought, or the actions stripping Jewish colleagues of their positions. Those who spoke up found themselves out of a job.

After the war, Julius Ebbinghaus, a philosophy professor who had lost his position for speaking out, reflected on what had happened—and what didn't. "'The German universities failed, while there was still time, to oppose publicly with all their power the destruction of knowledge and of the democratic state. They failed to keep the beacon of freedom and right burning during the night of tyranny.'"

Not all Germans were willing to go along with this.

Christian theologian Dietrich Bonhoeffer, who would later be hanged for his role in the failed July 1944 plot to kill Hitler, belonged to a free-thinking family. His elderly grandmother Julie pushed past storm troopers to shop at a Jewish store in 1933. Bonhoeffer consistently spoke out against the Nazis.

But for most, the pressure to conform was intense. And children often followed what their parents did. To Sebastian Haffner it felt as if the air over the entire nation had become poisonous and choking. When the Nazis took over, he felt shocked, overwhelmed, and powerless against a regime whose policies he could not support. But he wasn't sure what he could do about it. Political opposition to the Nazis had collapsed; he felt that to try to resist as an individual would be suicide.

Haffner thought many non-Nazi Germans like himself had simply decided to look the other way, or cut themselves off, like someone unwilling to step outside the four walls of a room. They tried to pretend nothing bad was happening. "The temptation to do this was great, even for me—and many others gave in to it. Thank God, my attempt to seal myself off failed from the outset."

Instead, Haffner fell in love with a Jewish woman. Marriage between Jews and non-Jews was made illegal in 1935. So in 1938, Haffner and his fiancée escaped to England, where they married and had two children.

After the war, he returned to Germany, where he became a successful author and journalist. Following his death in 1999 at the age of ninety-one, his son discovered that in 1939 Haffner had written a memoir of his life under the Nazis. It was published in 2000 with the title *Defying Hitler*.

HATE IS PUT INTO US

Love also changed the life of one young German typist and avid reader—and may have saved it. Edith Rosenthal met a young man named Paul Lewandowski (later he changed his last name to Lavender) at a dance in 1934. Paul had been fired from his job for being Jewish, just as Edith eventually lost her position at I.G. Farben, a company that became increasingly supportive of Nazi policies.

Paul had moved to Amsterdam in the Netherlands, where he'd found a job as a door-to-door salesman for coffee and tea. By the mid-1930s, Edith's family was debating how to leave Germany. Her parents had begun to contact relatives in other countries to find help with the immigration process. When Edith told Paul she was thinking of going to her mother's distant cousin in South Africa, he wrote back immediately. "'South Africa? You're coming to Amsterdam, and I'm going to marry you. Do you want to marry me?'"

Edith said yes! She was able to get to Amsterdam, where the couple was married by a rabbi on November 3, 1935. Many Jews initially felt safe living in the Netherlands, not realizing that Hitler would invade that country in May 1940. But Paul didn't feel safe and wanted to go to America. He had relatives who helped the young couple get to the United States in 1937. While Edith's brother and parents managed to escape, Paul's mother and twin brother, who'd moved to Amsterdam from Germany, were murdered in the Holocaust.

Edith and Paul Lavender eventually settled in Portland, Oregon. Years later, the city of Wiesbaden, Germany, invited Edith and her husband to return for a special visit as part of reconciliation efforts after the war. During their time in the city, Edith went to Mr. Schwab's old bookstore.

Mr. Schwab had passed away, but Edith met his son. "When I introduced myself, he said, 'Ah, I remember my father telling me there was a young Jewish girl who always came and he was friends with her and he gave her a box of books. Is that you?'"

It was. The man's son continued the tradition and presented Edith with a book.

As for the company Edith had worked for, during World War II, I.G. Farben became notorious for using labor from Auschwitz death camp to make its products, including poison gas used to kill one million people in gas chambers.

Paul and Edith both told their stories before they passed away in their nineties in 2005, after nearly seventy years of marriage. When asked about his message for future generations, Paul said, "Hate is something that is put into us. A baby is not born with hate. A baby is born with love. . . . I think after twenty centuries we should have developed further in trying to do away with division and promote togetherness, understanding, love."

LOOK, LISTEN, REMEMBER: Interviews with Edith and Paul Lavender are available online at the Oregon Jewish Museum and Center for Holocaust Education. You can read Edith's account of secretly receiving books here: http://www.ojmche.org /oral-history-interviews/edith-lavender-1993?A=Search Result&SearchID=5120418&ObjectID=5304275& ObjectType=35.

Hitler Youth boys marching with flags in the mid-1930s.

HITLER YOUTH

Under the Nazis, fewer young people enrolled in universities to get an education. But millions joined the Hitler Youth. Youth groups were extremely popular in Germany. Adolf Hitler took advantage of this tradition in 1926 when he formed the Hitler Youth organization to recruit young Germans to his incendiary ideas. Hitler Youth promised to deliver a sense of belonging, excitement, and adventure.

Jewish children were not allowed to join. Hedi Ballantyne was half Jewish. At school, Hedi's friends all wore swastika lapel pins. Many had joined the Hitler Youth. Hedi didn't like being excluded and feeling different from her friends.

When Hedi asked her mother about joining, her mother tried to explain that Hitler Youth wasn't just another group like scouts. "'You are half Jewish and to Hitler, who hates Jews, that's the same as being Jewish.'"

In fact, Hitler Youth was a sophisticated propaganda effort—a way to influence millions of young Germans to become Nazis. By 1932, members of the Hitler Youth were playing a role in politics, and organizing rallies and marches to get candidates from the Nazi Party elected to the Reichstag, Germany's parliament. By 1939, more than seven million German young people were part of the group.

Not every young person accepted the hero worship

and racist ideas of Hitler. In the summer of 1942, students at the University of Munich formed an anti-Nazi group called the White Rose.

One founding member was Hans Scholl, who had once been part of the Hitler Youth. Hans and his sister Sophie were arrested for distributing anti-Hitler leaflets. Along with their friend Christoph Probst, they were found guilty of treason and executed on February 22, 1943. A square at the University of Munich campus is named in their memory.

Members of the Hitler Youth marching.

Chapter Five

WHEN HATE
BECOMES LAW

Ruth

WE CHILDREN SCREAMED

"My teacher wore a brown uniform and expected us all to leap to our feet shooting out our right arm in the Hitler salute when he or any teacher entered the classroom," recalled Ruth David.

Ruth had started school in 1935 at age six; by then, the cult of Hitler had spread throughout Germany. "I knew my parents would not be keen for me to do this, but need not have had any qualms. I was told not to salute; I was to remain seated. Every time the class leapt up, I hung my head in shame. I was different and I had to live with it."

On the way home from school, other students threw stones at Ruth. She never told her parents. "I understood enough to realize that I could not appeal to an adult for help."

Ruth and her older sister Hannah switched to a Jewish school in a neighboring town. They traveled there in an old van, driven by one of their teachers. One day a local truck driver blocked the van's path. He came up to the stopped vehicle, clutching a piece of metal in his hand.

"Without a word, he proceeded to smash the windows of our van, behind which we children screamed and cowered," Ruth said. "Why did he do this? Had his colleagues in the [Nazi] party suggested it? Did he know he would derive pleasure from terrorizing young children? Was he going to brag to his drinking companions about this personal triumph over the Jews, as the men enjoyed their evening beer?"

While the attack went on, the driver sat still, afraid and helpless to fight back. Ruth's mother, who taught part-time in the school, was in the front passenger seat. "There is still a vivid picture of her in my memory: sitting next to the driver, she was looking straight ahead, her face rigid."

THE NUREMBERG LAWS

By the summer of 1935, violent attacks such as the one Ruth experienced were on the rise. That truck driver who attacked Ruth's school van probably didn't have orders from above. Nazi thugs like him often acted randomly and viciously all on their own. And, as Ruth saw for herself, there was little Jewish people could do. Complaining to the local police station didn't help: Those men were under the control of the Nazis too.

However, not all German citizens approved of this kind of violence. It wasn't that they supported Jews. Instead, people simply didn't like having their daily lives disrupted by unpleasant incidents. Historian Ian Kershaw observed, "What concerned people above all were the hooliganism, mob violence, distasteful scenes, and disturbances of order."

Hitler had used legal means to turn the Weimar democracy into a dictatorship. Now his response was to turn these random acts of Nazi violence into policy. The goal of the man who smashed the windows of a van carrying small children was to make life horrible so that Jews would leave the country.

Hitler supported that same goal. He made persecution the law of the land, enacting new restrictions that would cause problems for all Jewish people—and give the state itself permission to intimidate and punish.

In September 1935, at a Nazi convention in the city of Nuremberg, Hitler introduced the Nuremberg Laws, which formed the framework for additional anti-Semitic restrictions that followed.

• *Gesetz zum Schutze des Deutschen Blutes und der Deutschen Ehre* ("Law for the Protection of German Blood and German Honor"), also known as the Blood Protection Law. This banned marriage between Jewish and non-Jewish people. Jews were also forbidden from employing German women under the age of forty-five as servants. (This law implied that young Aryan women wouldn't be safe around Jewish men.)

• *Reichsbürgergesetz* ("Law of the Reich Citizen"). This law deprived Jews of their German citizenship. Instead, they were designated "subjects of the state," stripping Jews (defined as anyone with at least one Jewish grandparent) of the right to vote or the ability to hold public office.

The 1935 Nuremberg Laws were just part of the many restrictions that affected the lives and livelihoods of Jewish families throughout Germany. "LITTLE BY LITTLE. That's how the survivors of the Berlin Jewish community describe the Nazi attacks upon them," wrote historian Leonard Baker. "In 1933 the Nazis enacted forty-two laws restricting the Jews' rights to earn a living, to enjoy full citizenship, and to educate themselves. In 1934 there were nineteen such laws, twenty-nine in 1935, twenty-four in 1936, twenty-two in 1937, and seventy-eight in 1938."

Nazi laws and restrictions made life difficult in many ways. As we've seen, Jews were banned from universities; Jewish actors were dismissed from theaters; Jewish authors' works were rejected by publishers; and Jewish journalists were hard-pressed to find newspapers that would publish their writings.

Another new German law required that anyone Jewish had to have a *J* stamped on his or her passport. This *J* stamp law was developed in conjunction with the Swiss government, which wanted to identify and restrict Jewish refugees trying to cross the border into Switzerland. In addition, Jews were required to have traditional Jewish names so they could be readily identified by the authorities. If they didn't, they were required to add one legally: Sara for girls and Israel for boys.

In this way, Hitler was able to establish a legal framework to deprive Jews of their rights and made further persecutions possible. His first goal was to rid Germany of Jews. Beginning around mid-1941, this would become the "Final Solution," the Nazi plan for the brutal, state-sponsored murder of six million Jews, which included a million children, in death camps.

But evidence of Hitler's ultimate plan was there years before. In 1937, Hitler described his strategy this way: "'I don't straight away want violently to demand an opponent to fight. I don't say "fight" because I want to fight. Instead, I say, "I want to destroy you!" And now let skill help me to maneuver you so far into the corner that you can't strike any blow. And then you get the stab into the heart.'"

Ruth
SHE HAD LOVED ME

Ruth David's family had long employed a Catholic woman named Mina Dümig to help Ruth's mother around the house. To Ruth, Mina was like a second mother. And Mina, who was alone, loved the Oppenheimer children like her own.

Mina was under forty-five; and at first, Ruth recalled, she simply ignored the new Nuremberg law that forbid her from working for a Jewish family. "When the order came out, via the town crier, that 'Aryans' were no longer allowed to work for Jews, she shrugged her shoulders and ignored what she considered a stupidity," Ruth remembered. And when the Nazis paid her a visit and asked her to leave, Mina "swore at them loud and long and they slunk away."

Despite her protests, Mina was eventually forced to comply. This was especially hard on Ruth. "I could not come to terms with her leaving. . . . She had cared for me and loved me, and I loved her devotedly in return. I was slowly beginning to understand what genuine injustice was."

Mina never turned her back on those she loved. Later, when events in November 1938 made life in their small town impossible, Ruth's family decided to leave for Mannheim, a larger city. When the time came to move, Ruth and her little sister, Feo, fell ill with whooping cough and had to be left behind until they got better. Their elderly aunt and Uncle Gustav, who was disabled, weren't easily able to care for them.

"So Mina, who never lost touch, came back, strictly against Nazi orders," Ruth recalled. "I think the local guardians of the law were too scared of her to intervene. She bought food for us in the shops we were not allowed to enter. She looked after and comforted two very frightened little girls.

"Mina continued to stay in touch with my parents. . . . She must have been a comfort to them in a world from which they had lost all their non-Jewish friends, where the ordinary population was entitled to commit random hostile and brutal acts."

Marianne
HE FELT GERMAN
THROUGH AND THROUGH

The new laws also changed life for Marianne Elsley and her family. Her mother had been a doctor who treated patients from an office in their house in Rostock; Marianne's father was a respected and hardworking judge. When the Nazis put restrictions on Jewish doctors, Marianne's mother had to stop practicing medicine. Later Marianne's father lost his position because it was a civil service job.

Still, Marianne's parents kept hoping the Nazi Party would be thrown out. Marianne's father could not bring himself to turn his back on the country he loved. "He was thoroughly steeped in the German ways of thinking and felt German through and through," Marianne said. "For this reason he could not be persuaded to leave his country until it was too late; he could not believe that such horrors should happen to him in his own land."

One day, Marianne and her parents went into a local shop. Marianne said later they simply hadn't noticed a new sign saying Jews weren't welcome. "We were thunderstruck when the proprietor turned us out, shouting abuse. My father was, of course, well-known in our small town as an official of the local court, and this was quite horrific for him."

Marianne had been friends with the shop owner's daughter. But friendship didn't seem to matter anymore. "The time had come to move to Berlin," Marianne said. "By now, in twos and threes, our friends and relatives were leaving their homeland, settling in America

Beginning with a major boycott on April 1, 1933, anti-Semitic measures harmed many Jewish businesses. Here, in 1933 Berlin, SA men hold banners reading: GERMANS! DEFEND YOURSELVES! DO NOT BUY FROM JEWS!

and England and sending for more members of the family. My father still could not face up to this idea. His Fatherland would come to its senses; he dreaded the idea of having to be a stranger in a foreign land. . . . The move to Berlin seemed the answer for the moment."

Marianne would attend a Jewish school in Berlin. Maybe things would get better.

Leslie
PRELUDE TO TERROR

Like so many others, Leslie Brent encountered trouble at school. In 1935, when he was ten, Leslie switched to a school where he could study English and French.

Leslie's English teacher was a committed Nazi Party member who often wore a uniform to school.

"It was he, ironically, who taught me English, and it went strongly against his grain that I proved to be one of his best pupils," Leslie remembered. His teacher would've been surprised to learn that within a few years, his Jewish student would be speaking in English on a BBC radio program heard by millions.

Leslie was the only Jewish student in his school. He had to dodge snowballs and stones as he walked home. He ran a lot, and the practice paid off. Much to the dismay of his Nazi teacher, Leslie won a sprint race at a sports day.

But then someone scribbled anti-Christian remarks on the chalkboard. It didn't matter that Leslie was innocent: He was blamed. In the winter of 1936, when Leslie was eleven, his parents decided to send him to live at a Jewish boys' orphanage in the large city of Berlin. He wasn't an orphan, of course. But his parents knew the director and thought that there Leslie could receive an education without being harassed.

That move changed Leslie's life—and probably saved it.

Leslie's new home was a historic orphanage that had been founded in 1882 in a suburb of Berlin to house Jewish children fleeing from pogroms, organized attacks on Jews, in Russia. Although the people in the orphanage were kind, it was quite an adjustment to move from family life into a dormitory with other boys.

Leslie's parents and sister soon made the move to Berlin as well, hoping they could blend in better in a large city. But they struggled to survive financially. "My father was reduced to earning a pittance by working in a timber factory," Leslie said. "I saw my parents at weekends and they tried hard to behave normally. Looking back at those fleeting moments of contact, I can only marvel at their bravery and fortitude."

Then, in the late summer of 1938, a frightening incident took place. "The orphanage was stormed by a mob that had suddenly and mysteriously gathered outside," Leslie said. "The heavy front doors having been hastily locked, the rabble attempted to gain entrance through the gate leading into the courtyard at the back."

Leslie and his friend Fred Gerstl ran upstairs and found a place to hide in the darkness under the rafters of the roof. "There we stayed with beating hearts until everything became eerily quiet." Thanks to one of the teachers who distracted the mob, most of the building remained untouched, though the ground floor and basement were ransacked.

Later, Leslie wondered if the incident was simply a rehearsal for the terror that was to come.

THE SIGNS WERE ALL THERE

Little by little Jewish families throughout Germany grappled with how to survive under Nazi rule that seemed to make each day harder than the next. Some parents still hoped the Nazis couldn't remain in power for long. They hoped to ride out the hard times. Everyone worried about their children; they wanted to keep them safe and give them a better life.

Werner Angress was older than the children who left on the Kindertransport. But, thanks to his father, who did not survive the Holocaust, Werner escaped to the United States. His path was a long one.

BUT OF COURSE WE DIDN'T KNOW

Werner Angress lived with his family in Berlin. Born in June 1920, he was almost thirteen when he began to see columns of Hitler Youth and brownshirts marching everywhere in his city. "Later in the United States, I was often asked why we didn't pack up and leave the country immediately after the Nazis took power in 1933. If we had known what was in store for us, my family and probably the majority of German Jews would have done just that. But of course we didn't know. . . .

"We waited, tried to adjust, hoped the Nazis would change their minds about the Jews, and otherwise went about our daily activities at work, at home, and at school," he said. "Papa was reluctant to take his wife and children to a foreign country, where his future would have been uncertain."

When the government announced a boycott of Jewish businesses on April 1, 1933, Werner's mother decided to lodge a protest in her own way. She took her three sons to a sewing goods store owned by two Jewish women. She sent Werner and his brother in, one after another, to make small purchases of buttons and thread. Then she herself went in with her youngest son.

When it was his turn, Werner's heart pounded as he went past the guard, but luckily the man didn't stop any of them. "If I had been older and wiser, maybe the day of the boycott would have opened my eyes. I was convinced that sooner or later the government would recognize what good Germans we Jews were and change its attitude toward us."

Werner went on, "Naïve as we (and many adults) were then, we firmly believed that all we had to do was prove to the new German government that in all our being, thinking, and actions we were German and would remain German. When the Nazis understood this, they would have to accept us into the broad front of 'German renewal.'"

This way of thinking, Werner later reflected, wasn't unusual at the start. "At least during the beginning phase of the Third Reich, many Jewish leaders hoped that the new German rulers might be persuaded to drop their anti-Semitic attitude and measures."

Those hopes would come to nothing.

Shortly after the Nuremberg Laws were announced in 1935, Werner's father took him for a walk to discuss his future. Werner would soon leave school. At the time, Werner never imagined that someday he'd earn a PhD and become a distinguished professor of history. Werner's father advised him to look for a practical profession. There was a good reason for this.

"In a low voice that trembled with stifled agitation, Papa told me I could no longer remain in Germany," Werner remembered. "The Nazis had instituted the Nuremberg Laws to take away the Jews' rights and honor. The younger generation to which my brothers and I belonged no longer had a future in our country and thus had to think about emigrating." Werner's father thought his own generation would have to stick it out. But if Werner could find some sort of practical training, it might improve his chances to emigrate and earn a living abroad.

A few weeks later, Werner's father saw a notice about a Jewish farm training program called Gross Breesen near the Polish border. Here and in other places like it, young Jewish students learned agriculture and carpentry—skills that would make them valued workers in a new country. The program directors also actively worked to find opportunities for the young people to leave Germany.

Werner applied and was accepted. In May 1936, he moved to Gross Breesen. He enjoyed the work and made close friends. But in October 1937, he received a mysterious postcard from his father, summoning him home to Berlin for the weekend. When Werner arrived, he found out his father no longer believed sticking it out was possible for anyone. He had hatched a daring escape plan for them all to go to the Netherlands.

I DON'T STITCH JEWS

John Fieldsend was born on September 11, 1931. His original name was Hans Heinrich Feige; his family called him Heini. John lived with his brother, Arthur, and their parents in Dresden, Germany. John had faced bullying and taunts not only in school but also in the playground near their apartment block.

"My brother and I regularly played with the many other children from the apartments and had a great time together," John recalled. "However, quite suddenly, the other children started to name-call my brother and me as dirty Jews—and so the bullying began. We were kicked, punched and spat upon."

When he was five or six, John fell and got a deep cut on his forehead. His parents rushed him to their usual doctor, who turned them away, saying, "'That needs stitching . . . I don't stitch Jews.'"

John's father realized the situation was becoming more dangerous by the day. "So late one night, without any goodbyes, we simply got into our car, with only the most basic of our possessions, and drove through the night to my mother's parents' home in Czechoslovakia. Fortunately, because we carried so few possessions, we did not raise any suspicions with the border guards."

The family settled in a small town, but peace didn't last long. In an attempt to avoid another war with Germany, there was only mild resistance when Hitler launched his expansion plans, first into Austria in 1938, and then into parts of Czechoslovakia in October 1938, followed by the rest of the country in March 1939.

When Germans moved into John's town, they confiscated his family's car. Once, when John was helping his father cut down a diseased plum tree in their garden, he heard heavy footsteps coming up the path. An SS officer (like the SA, the SS, or Schutzstaffel, was a Nazi paramilitary group) approached and demanded to know what they were doing.

"And at the blink of an eye the simple act of cutting down a diseased tree turned into a frightening SS interrogation," said John. "It is something that I will remember for the rest of my life."

WHERE TO?

Ruth Sass Glaser grew up in Düsseldorf, Germany, where she was born in 1919. As the Nazis cemented control, life became more and more difficult.

"Every few months a new situation presented itself and had to be overcome like another hurdle," she recalled. "The Führer kept on infiltrating the minds of the German people and re-educating them and teaching them to hate. The economic situation began to improve, which gave him more power with every passing day. As time went by, my parents became aware of the fact that they no longer could take vacation trips around the country. The hotels did not want Jewish clientele."

At school, Ruth boldly told one teacher she didn't want to be present whenever he made rude comments about Jews. In biology, she had to sit through lessons claiming human beings who had Aryan blood were superior to all others.

"While I was in school I felt like fighting all this, but as soon as I was home I felt scared and worried what it would lead to and it became clear that I was not wanted in this country." When Ruth tried to talk to her parents, she found they were in denial. "I told my parents about my experiences in school and urged them to make plans to leave. They looked at me bewildered. How could they pack up and leave everything that was close and dear to them, and where to? How could they start a new business in a strange country, not knowing the language, and which country was willing to let them immigrate?"

THE ANSCHLUSS—GERMAN TAKEOVER OF AUSTRIA

On March 12, 1938, the Anschluss took place. This was the annexation of Austria into Nazi Germany. Unlike other countries, Austria welcomed the Germans. As Ruth David noted, "The Austrians were even more anti-Semitic than the Germans." Austrian Jews came to feel the full brunt of Nazi restrictions and persecution tactics immediately.

Seven-year-old Harry Heber and his sister, Ruth, three years older, were living in Innsbruck, Austria,

Hitler accepts the ovation of the Reichstag after announcing the "peaceful" acquisition of Austria. It set the stage to annex the Czechoslovakian Sudetenland, largely inhabited by a German-speaking population. Berlin, March 1938.

when the annexation took place. "My father sold bed linen and textiles from a shop near the old market square," he recalled. "My mother made duvets, and filled them with goose feathers in the yard. When the wind caught the feathers they'd swirl through the air, and I'd run through them as if they were snow."

He remembers standing on the main street when the Germans marched in. "Soldiers paraded through the town with a brass band. Within days, the word 'Jude' had been smeared across the windows of my father's shop."

The family moved to Vienna, but the situation there was no better. The city had turned against its Jewish residents. "You couldn't go out," Harry said. "You weren't permitted to sit in public parks. Teachers lost their jobs. Children couldn't go to school. Everyone got panicked. They could sense what was going to come." Harry's father would go every day and wait in long lines to get the paperwork needed to emigrate. But he never got past the door.

LONGING TO LEAVE

Edith Liebenthal remembered the day the Nazis invaded Vienna, where she'd been born in 1924. Edith was an only child; her father, who'd served in World War I, worked for a bank. Her mother ran her own business, screen-printing scarves.

Like other children growing up before the Nazis, Edith had wonderful memories of her early childhood. She especially loved summer visits to her grandparents on their farm in Slovakia, where they had a calf that licked her with its sandpaper tongue, and fields full of wheat and corn. Edith liked to gather blue cornflowers and red poppies. She liked to watch for the mail, which arrived on a horse-drawn wagon.

In March 1938, the Anschluss changed everything. "Vienna was quite literally overnight converted into a city of jubilation; the troops, the SA and SS were welcomed as liberators and most everyone displayed the swastika pin," said Edith. "I can still feel the shock and disbelief when I realized that our neighbors, most of my teachers, the storekeepers—all had belonged to the Nazi party.

"For a short while life went on as usual. I was allowed to finish the school year with the understanding that I could not continue into the next grade, as I had already turned fourteen. Eventually my father lost his job, without any kind of severance pay, of course. My mother was also forced to wind down her business; her customers were no longer allowed to buy from her," said Edith later.

"The search to escape to freedom was on."

It was hard to find a country that would let them in. Edith's mother had registered them at an American consulate. She'd managed to locate an old friend in the United States who was willing to file an affidavit for them. "The requirement was that a U.S. citizen had to issue a sworn statement to the effect that the people he was sponsoring would not become a burden to the state."

There were also quotas, with only a certain number of people allowed in each year. Edith's family knew it would take one or two years before their number came up. Meanwhile, "the situation was getting worse from day to day; atrocities against Jews were commonplace. We were stuck in Vienna."

THE SIGNS WERE ALL THERE

Along with his parents and sister, Alfred "Freddie" Traum often listened to Hitler's speeches on the radio in their Vienna apartment. Each speech seemed to be endless, he remembered. "It went on and on for ages—mostly ranting and raving. . . . I couldn't concentrate on what he was saying, but noticed the expressions on my parents' faces. My mother's eyes were moist near to tears; my father sat stone faced. But deep down I knew that whatever Hitler was saying was not good for us Jews.

"The worsening situation for Jews living under Nazi rule was already very much in evidence through restrictions, persecutions, fathers abruptly disappearing

German girls posing outside their school with a swastika. Among them is a girl named Lilli Eckstein, who was later expelled from the school for being Jewish.

without warning," said Freddie. "In some cases they reappeared, after several months, and were given just days to leave the country. We learned later that they had been incarcerated at Dachau or Buchenwald. The signs were all there. There was no future for Jews under Nazi rule. The only question remaining was where to go?"

GO HOME

Lisa Leist Seiden enjoyed her school in Vienna. But one day, when she was nine, Lisa's teacher took her aside, gave her a hug, and kissed her. With tears in her eyes, the teacher told the little girl, "'Go home, you can't be here anymore, go and don't come back.'"

Lisa tried to think what she'd done wrong. Her teacher only repeated the instruction and said Lisa should ask her mother to explain. Her mother told her, "'It's because we are Jews.'"

Lisa was shocked and confused. How could that be? Before this, her friends had just been friends; she hadn't distinguished between those who were Jewish and those who weren't. "Nothing in my appearance, manner or life style had made me feel different from the other children of my school," said Lisa. "We wore the same kind of clothes, ate the same kind of food, played the same kind of games. There was no difference between us.

"But soon the things which were happening around us, took care to 'mark the Difference' and the punishment of not being able to continue in my school was but the first, followed by others, deeper, darker and completely irreparable."

The Nazis targeted Jewish children early in Hitler's rule. On April 25, 1933, a law called the German Act against the Overcrowding of Schools and Universities mandated the percentage of Jewish students who could be enrolled in a state-run school. Jewish students who remained faced bullying not only from fellow students but from teachers too. In 1938, all Jewish children were expelled from state-run schools.

THE LAST CAREFREE SUMMER

Hedi Ballantyne had loved spending summer vacations with her parents in a farmhouse in the Austrian countryside. That all ended one night in August 1938, when she heard shouts outside her open window. The next morning, her mother announced they had to leave immediately. Hedi began to cry. She didn't want to go. But there was no choice: A group of Hitler Youth had found out they were there.

"As I kneeled on the back seat of the bus and looked back to the little village and the small group of people standing there waving, tears streamed down my face again as I thought, 'This is the last time I see this place where I have been so happy.'"

That fall, back at school in Vienna, things got worse. Her classmates began to scorn and taunt her. "As I walked home from school some children threw things at me. 'Jew girl, Jew girl!' they yelled. They grabbed my school books and threw them in the street."

And then came November 1938.

Part Two

THE TIPPING POINT

1938

I don't think evil begins in a sudden enormous rush. It starts in small ways and grows. It's like water finding its way to the sea. It just grows and grows and grows and grows—if you let it.

—**THEA FELIKS EDEN**

Hebrew prayer books and other Jewish religious texts damaged by fire at the synagogue in Bobenhausen II, District Vogelsberg, during Kristallnacht in November 1938.

November 10, 1938
Berlin, Germany

It is late at night—I want to try to write down, with a trembling hand, today's events, events that have engraved themselves in flaming letters on my heart. I want to write them down for my child, so that someday he can read how they destroyed his life.

I want to relate my experience—at this midnight hour, sitting alone and trembling at my desk, groaning painfully like a wounded animal—I want to write, in order not to scream out loud in the still of the night.

Yesterday a murder was committed in Paris—a Polish Jew shot a secretary at the German embassy.

Now all Jews must atone for it!

—HERTHA NATHORFF

Kristallnacht
THE NIGHT OF BROKEN GLASS

In late October 1938, the Nazis expelled more than twelve thousand Jews of Polish background. Although they'd been living legally in Germany, some for many years, they didn't have German blood, which was held against them, along, of course, with being Jewish. Some had children born in Germany. It didn't matter. Germany decided to deport them. These Jewish families were forced out of their homes suddenly; they were allowed to take just a few belongings.

The families were herded onto trains that rumbled through the cold to the Polish border. Once again, cruel laws were used to target Jews. After Germany had annexed Austria earlier in 1938, Poland had worried that thousands of Jews who were living in Austria would decide to return to Poland. To prevent that, the Polish government put restrictions on people who were living outside of Poland but still held Polish passports. Basically, people who had been living abroad for five years or more would need to get their passports revalidated. In early October, the deadline was set for October 30. This meant that overnight, thousands of people lost their Polish citizenship, and as Jews, the Nuremberg Laws of 1935 had deprived them of their German citizenship, making them subjects of the state.

Poland did take back about four thousand of the

Jewish refugees expelled by Germany. But everyone else became stranded on the border. Their only shelter were some old stables in Zbaszyn, where conditions soon became horrific.

The Grynszpan family was one of those expelled. But seventeen-year-old Herschel Grynszpan was living in Paris and wasn't with the rest of his family. His sister sent him a postcard to tell him what had happened to them. Enraged and upset, Grynszpan bought a pistol on November 6. The next day, he went to the German embassy, claiming to have a document to deliver. He managed to reach the office of the third secretary, a man named Ernst vom Rath. There, claiming to speak for those who had been deported, he fired five shots at the official.

On Wednesday evening, November 9, on a day when Hitler was commemorating the anniversary of his 1923 Beer Hall Putsch, Rath died of his injuries. (Herschel Grynszpan was arrested and imprisoned. His exact fate is unknown.)

The Nazis decided to use the German official's death as the rationale for a massive pogrom. Hitler and Joseph Goebbels, his minister of propaganda, deployed storm troopers in acts of retaliation against Jews in cities and towns all over Germany and Austria. Police stations were ordered not to interfere. If any Jewish victims complained, they were to be arrested. Firefighters were told to let synagogues burn but to save other properties nearby so long as they didn't belong to Jews.

In two days and nights, more than a thousand synagogues were burned or otherwise damaged. Rioters ransacked and looted thousands of Jewish businesses and killed at least ninety-one Jews. They broke windows and vandalized Jewish hospitals, homes, schools, and cemeteries. In the days that followed, some thirty thousand Jewish males aged sixteen to sixty were arrested and sent to three camps: Dachau, Buchenwald, and Sachsenhausen, some for days or weeks, some for longer.

The pogrom was given a poetic name: Kristallnacht, or crystal night, because of the amount of broken glass on the streets. (Today it is also called Pogromnacht.) But there was no poetry in the terror of the night of broken glass.

Chapter Six

THE NINTH OF NOVEMBER

In November 1938, Hannele Zürndorfer was about to turn thirteen. She lived on the outskirts of Düsseldorf, Germany, with her parents and little sister, Lotte. Hannele's family observed the Jewish religious holidays, but Hannele also grew up with a Christmas tree. Her father, a successful publisher and theater critic, explained that having a tree helped their Catholic maid, Anna, feel more at home. But Hannele suspected her father simply loved festivals and celebrations of all kinds and enjoyed making magic for his two daughters.

At Christmas, Hannele's parents would trim the tree in secret and then open the door. "I was aware only of a magic glow at the far end," she said. "There the tall, dark green spruce stood transformed. It was set with a trembling mantle of white candles; glistening strands of silver hair [tinsel] flowed over the branches and the top was crowned with a large silver star."

There were also candles to celebrate Hanukkah, the Jewish Festival of Lights. "The old brass candelabrum, the Menorah, that had been passed down through several generations, was brought out and polished till it shone. It had eight main arms and a small ninth arm in front for the 'servant' candle, from which the others had to be lit, one candle more each night," said Hannele. When all were lit, "their light seemed to grow and suffuse the whole room."

For Passover, Hannele's family might have twenty people gathered for dinner to commemorate the exodus of the Jews from Egypt. "There was the best china and silver, stiffly starched napkins and tablecloth and beautiful, cut crystal wine glasses in sparkling colors. By the side of my father stood a huge platter containing ten little dishes for the bitter herbs, spices and condiments, the harsh or bitter taste of each representing one of the ten plagues . . . Each person had a piece of matzoh (a kind of water biscuit) representing the unleavened bread of the first Passover."

Hannele also enjoyed going shopping in the lively city with her mother. "My favorite shop was the delicatessen, kept by an oddly assorted couple. She was a tiny, dark bird of a woman with black eyes like a sparrow and he was a fair giant, slow and kind. Both of them smiled a great deal . . . Nearly all my favorite foods came out of their barrels: pickled herrings, pickled gherkins and smoked eel." Another much-loved shop was the bakery, where Hannele could choose crisp white rolls or currant buns with cinnamon.

After Hitler became chancellor, a feeling of gloom seemed to permeate everything. Hannele noticed her parents seemed more serious; adult conversations would suddenly stop when she and her sister approached. Her old friends treated her differently. "At first I only sensed that I was less welcome in the street games; then some of the other children became actively hostile, teasing and baiting me and pushing me about when I was on roller skates; so that I no longer liked going out to play."

Eventually, Hannele had to leave her old school and go to a private Jewish one more than an hour away by tram. Her father lost his job. She began to feel real fear. "I wanted to shut out the grey, fearsome streets with jackbooted Brownshirts who stamped about like robots, marching, shouting, saluting, red-faced, with wild and bloodshot eyes. At least, that is how they appeared to me. Danger was outside. At home we were safe—I thought."

Until November 9.

"It must have been three or four o'clock in the morning, when suddenly I was ripped out of my sleep by the sound of smashing crockery and glass! On and on it went," recalled Hannele. "At first I thought I must be dreaming still; it was an impossible sound in the dark and sleeping house."

Hannele bolted upright, then she grabbed little Lotte, and the sisters flew to their parents' room in terror. "Seconds later there burst into this room a horde of

A private Jewish home in Vienna, Austria, vandalized during the Kristallnacht pogrom on November 10, 1938.

violent monsters, their faces contorted into raving masks of hatred, some red, some pale, all screaming and shouting, eyes rolling, teeth bared, wild hands flailing, jackboots kicking," Hannele said.

"They were wielding axes, sledgehammers, stones and knives. They rushed about the room smashing, throwing, trampling. It seemed to me that there were hundreds of them bursting through the door, though I believe there were, in fact, only a dozen."

Horrified, Hannele watched as her father, still in his nightshirt, tried to protect a treasured landscape painting. Ignoring his desperate pleas, a Nazi dug his knife deep into the canvas. "Now fear became a living thing, fear for the life and safety of my parents, who represented my own safety," Hannele wrote later. "It was like drowning."

There was just a small pinpoint of light in this dark and horrible night. One of the men came up to the terrified children and whispered, "'Children don't look, don't look children. Hide your eyes. I am sorry. I had to do it.'"

Slowly, that man drew the others away, leaving Hannele's father slumped and weeping. The apartment and all their lovely things had been ruined: the piano ripped apart, every painting torn to shreds, her mother's collection of china cups smashed. The Nazis had torn the legs off tables and chairs, hacked at the carpets, torn out the pages of books, and smashed windows.

When first light came, the dazed family wandered through the ruins. Was it only their home that had been attacked? Was it safe to go out? What was happening?

KRISTALLNACHT

DON'T CRY

Each family's experience of Kristallnacht and its aftermath was different. Lisa Leist Seiden remembered men coming into her house, located in a quiet suburb of Vienna. Her family lived on the top floor of a three-story house, with access to a terraced rooftop where they made giant snowmen in winter; they also had a pretty back garden with a cherry tree and roses. It was a lovely place to live.

But that night footsteps echoed in the hall and the men burst in, pushing her and her mother down the stairs and into the street, where the brownshirts had scrawled the words *Jewish Swine*. The Nazis brought out a bucket and hand brush and forced Lisa's mother to scrub away the words. They made Lisa stand by her side and watch. When it was done, the brownshirts just laughed and wrote the same insult again, farther down the street. And once again they made Lisa's mother clean it.

"This went on and on for what seemed an eternity," Lisa remembered. Once, her mother looked straight at her and shot her a warning glance. "Her silent message was, 'Don't cry!'

"I didn't."

A few days later, Lisa and her mother saw SS troopers waiting at the end of the street. Lisa knew why they

Jewish men are forced to sweep the pavement in the town square of Raciaz, Poland, with short brooms.

were there. One of their neighbors, a non-Jewish shopkeeper, had told Lisa's mother the Nazis had been into her shop, asking about Lisa's father.

Lisa's father didn't want to be arrested. Instead of coming home, he hid under a small bridge near their house. Lisa and her brother had played there before: It was a secret hollow, full of trees and thick shrubs.

Lisa was the one who brought her father food. Her mother thought that as a small child she'd be the most inconspicuous, the least likely to be stopped. To reach her father, Lisa had to climb over their garden wall and go out the back way. She had to try to act normal if she met any German soldiers. When she reached the bridge, Lisa learned to slip into the hiding place as quickly as possible. In addition to food, Lisa carried messages from her mother.

"'I cannot write them down for you, it's too dangerous,'" her mother instructed. "'You must memorize them and repeat them to Papa; he must know that I am doing everything to get the Permit so that we can all leave the country as soon as possible.'"

Lisa was frightened, but she did everything exactly right. "The encounters with my father in that cold, dark burrow under the bridge will remain engraved like tongues of flame in the back of my mind, impossible to be forgotten," she wrote later. She never forgot how sad and desolate he looked. "Sometimes I still see him in my dreams, just as he was then. . . . I would throw myself into his arms, not understanding, not believing what was happening."

Her father tried to reassure her that all would be well. But he was caught and sent to Dachau. Lisa's family was fortunate, more fortunate than millions of others. Although it would be eight long years, Lisa would see her father again.

FIRST THEY BREAK THE WINDOWS

Frieda Stolzberg Korobkin was only five when Hitler annexed Austria in March 1938. That fall, Frieda and her nine-year-old brother, Ephraim, were throwing snowballs near their home in Vienna when, quite by accident, Ephraim hit a boy who happened to be passing by. The boy was wearing black jackboots and the outfit of a Hitler Youth. He and two of his friends took their anger out on little Frieda, piling snow on her head and taunting her.

"The Vienna of my childhood contained no waltzes or polkas, no romantic visions, either real or imagined," said Frieda. "One of my first vivid recollections, chilling in every sense, is being buried in the snow by three of Hitler's young hooligans."

By this time, the Nazis had closed their Jewish school, forcing Frieda and her three siblings to stay home in the family's frigid apartment. Frieda's father, a devout Jewish scholar who had taught in the school, tried to keep warm as he pored over his books. Frieda remembered him wearing his overcoat and drinking endless glasses of hot tea.

Just as the Nazis had made Lisa Leist Seiden's

mother scrub the streets, they forced Frieda's parents to do the same. Nazis also burned her father's prayer books, throwing them into a bonfire while non-Jewish neighbors cheered. At one point, Frieda realized that the building's janitor and his daughter, Inge, were jeering along with the others. Inge had once been her friend. But friendship had disappeared.

Frieda's mother ran a small grocery shop, which the brownshirts stormed too. "First they break the windows, then they ransack the shelves. My parents are forced to sweep up the broken glass and debris. There is no more food left," Frieda said.

As the synagogue in Ober-Ramstadt, Germany, burns during Kristallnacht, firefighters instead save a nearby house. Local residents watch as the synagogue is destroyed. November 9–10, 1938.

Frieda's mother and her eldest sister, Erica, took saucepans and waited in line at a Jewish community center to get meals for the family. Hearing that healthy Jewish men were being rounded up and arrested, Frieda's mother put her husband to bed and—though Frieda was never sure how her mother did it—managed to make him look and feel ill and hot. When the Nazis came for him, he appeared so sick they left without him.

COULD THIS BE POSSIBLE?

Rescue worker Norbert Wollheim was twenty-five and would come to play an important part in the Kindertransport. In November 1938, he'd just completed a welding course in Berlin. As he came out onto the street after his final examination, someone told him that synagogues were burning.

"I went to my synagogue, where I had been married, and I saw that the flames were coming out from the roof, from the cupola . . . and the fire engines were standing by doing nothing, only protecting the buildings next to it [so] that the fire shouldn't extend to them." Norbert stood frozen, listening to German people around him gleefully exclaim that this was what Jews deserved.

"I couldn't comprehend it. . . . I saw it but I couldn't digest, not intellectually and not emotionally. . . . I had read about pogroms in the Middle Ages. . . . but we were living in a modern age. . . . I had believed in the goodness of man. Could this be possible?"

ESCAPE OUT THE WINDOW

Fred M. Rosenbaum lived in Vienna, where he was born Fritz Rosenbaum. He was twelve in 1938 and on November 9 walked to school as usual. But the day was not a normal one.

"After about a half hour in the classroom, students dressed in Hitler youth uniforms asked all Jewish students to leave the classroom and stay in the hall," Fred said. The Jewish students were all pushed down into one basement room, and then the Hitler youth students began to beat them with belts and whips.

"Luckily, I was standing to the back of the room and noticed three or four small windows close to the top of the wall leading to the street," said Fred. "I jumped up to the window, pushed it open, and three of us escaped the room before the Hitler youth could catch us. I ran nonstop the two miles to my home, trying to find safety."

There was little safety to be had. "Thousands of Jews were put into concentration camps[;] stores [were] robbed, smashed, demolished[;] synagogues burned, and life as a Jew became even more unbearable than it ever had before."

A SCENE OF HORROR

Like Fred, Ernest G. Fontheim went to school as usual, taking the elevated train from his family's apartment in Berlin. "When I entered my classroom, some of my classmates were telling horror stories of what they had seen on their way to school, like smashed store windows of Jewish-opened shops, looting mobs, and even burning synagogues."

The students fell silent as their teacher entered. The teacher announced that the school would close for the day; the teachers couldn't guarantee the students' safety. He dismissed the pupils and warned them to go straight home, not to stop, and not to attract attention.

As he headed back home on the train, Ernest passed the Fasanenstrasse Synagogue, his family's place of worship. He saw smoke rising from it. On an impulse he couldn't explain, Ernest got off at the next stop and raced back to look.

"Firefighters were hosing down adjacent buildings. The air was filled with the acrid smell of smoke. I was wedged in the middle of a hostile crowd which was in an ugly mood shouting anti-Semitic slogans. I was completely hypnotized by the burning synagogue and was totally oblivious to any possible danger," he said later. "I thought of the many times I had attended services there and listened to the sermons all of

A synagogue burns in Wiesbaden, Germany.

which had fortified my soul during the difficult years of persecution."

And then Ernest witnessed the awful spectacle of mob violence. Someone shouted that a Jewish family lived in a ground-floor apartment across the street. The crowd moved toward the building, and people began beating their fists against the door.

"In my imagination I pictured a frightened family hiding in a room as far as possible from the entrance door—hoping and praying that the door would withstand, and I prayed with them. I vividly remember the crashing violent noise of splintering wood followed by deadly silence, then suddenly wild cries of triumph.

"An elderly bald-headed man was brutally pushed through the crowd while fists rained down on him from all sides." Ernest heard one man in the crowd shout a protest: "'How cowardly! So many against one!' He was immediately attacked by others."

The Jewish man from the apartment was pushed to the ground. A police car arrived, and he was put in and driven off. He would be arrested, not protected. Ernest turned away. "I left this scene of horror completely drained, incredulous. . . ."

Ernest Fontheim's parents and sister were arrested in 1942. Ernest, who was working at the time, was able to obtain false identity papers and later went into hiding along with his future wife, Margot, and her parents.

Local residents watch as flames consume the synagogue in the city of Opava (now part of the Czech Republic), set on fire during Kristallnacht.

View of the destroyed interior of the synagogue in Opava after Kristallnacht.

Just before they were turned in by a Nazi sympathizer, they were given new hiding places by an anti-Nazi German Army officer named Heinz Drossel and his family. Fontheim survived the war and moved to the United States, where he became a distinguished research scientist at the University of Michigan. Before his death, in 2008, Heinz Drossel was recognized for several acts of resistance to the Nazis during the war.

SHOELACES AND ASHES

Ursula Rosenfeld was a thirteen-year-old student living in a small town in Germany. Her school was opposite a synagogue. In class that November morning she heard noises and saw flames shooting up from the building: That synagogue had been set on fire too.

The Nazis had also ransacked the apartment of a Jewish family living nearby. "'They had thrown all their belongings out into the street, broken things. A little child's pram [stroller] was bashed to pieces. . . . And people were laughing and shouting and then they saw me and then they said, "There's another Jew! Let's throw her into the flames too!" And it was a moment in my life I shall never forget.

"'You couldn't imagine the atmosphere and the burning. . . . I don't even to this day remember how I got home. . . . I do remember seeing a truck with men, whom they obviously had arrested. . . . They had arrested my father too.

"'Well, eventually I got back home, and my mother and grandmother were absolutely distraught. . . . And that was the end of my school days, really. It was also the end of my family life. I didn't realize that was the end of everything really.'"

Ursula's father, like thousands of other Jewish men, was arrested and taken to Buchenwald concentration camp. Most of the men interned after Kristallnacht were able to return to their families. But not Ursula's father. Eventually, Ursula learned from others what happened.

When the Jewish men arrived, guards took the men's shoelaces away. "'My father was quite an outspoken person . . . and he protested and said, "You can't treat these old people like this." So they made an example of him and they beat him to death in front of everybody in order to instill terror and obedience. We heard a few days later that he had died of a heart attack, but this was the story the Nazis told all the families of the people they killed. . . .

"'The Nazis offered us my father's ashes in return for money. Eventually the urn came and we buried it in the Jewish cemetery. But, of course, whether it was his ashes one never knows.'"

Germans pass by the broken shop window of a Jewish-owned business that was destroyed during Kristallnacht.

Chapter Seven

THE TIPPING POINT

Ruth

THE BLOWS OF AN AXE

In Ruth David's village, the night of November 9 was quiet. But not the next. "I woke to thunderous knocking on the house door," said Ruth. "Apparently it was not opened quickly enough, as I could hear the blows of an axe and wood crashing, then shouting and screaming. . . . My sister Hannah came into my room. She had switched on the light but suddenly all was dark. We were terrified. Downstairs the voices were angry."

Ruth and Hannah fled barefoot down a back staircase and out into the night. Unsure where to go, they hid themselves in their father's car. From there, they peered out to see men smashing the windows of their house. Then, Ruth remembered, "The unexpected happened; a man whom we did not know came to the car . . . he stood in front of the car and said he would deal with anyone who tried to approach or harm us."

Time seemed to stop. "I cannot say today how long we remained in our hiding place; it seemed like many hours of shivering with cold and panic. I know that I experienced there, at the age of nine, the greatest fear I have ever known. I have been in some dangerous situations since, not least during air raids over the north of England, but nothing to match the cold terror of that night. We did not know what had taken place in the house, where our parents were, whether we could ever go back, or what would happen to us if we did."

When the intruders left, the girls climbed out of the car and hurried back inside to find their mother dazed and frightened. The attackers had hurled their dear uncle Gustav down the stairs; they'd also smashed his wheelchair, which he'd designed himself. Ruth's father and her older brother Ernst had been arrested and taken away to Buchenwald concentration camp.

"Today I am still trying to piece together the aftermath, but find it difficult," Ruth said years later. "I cannot remember how long it took to clear up the debris. Nor do I have any memories of helping, but I assume we all did. The windows and mirrors had been smashed, the pictures too. Every piece of furniture bore signs of the axe, though all was not totally destroyed. Curtains and bedding were ripped. The telephone had been torn out."

Sometimes small things stand out in our memories. For Ruth, it was her mother's heartbreak over one especially hurtful act. The mob had destroyed the fruits, vegetables, and jam she had preserved for the winter ahead. The long hours of work had been a labor of love. "Now each jar lay smashed on the floor, the liquid mess oozing blood red through the heaps of broken glass."

Ruth's family had lived in Fränkisch-Crumbach for several generations; her father had been a member of the local governing council; he'd helped to bring electricity to the village, improving daily life for all. Yet it had become too dangerous to stay.

"It was clear that continuing to live there would not only be difficult, it would become impossible. Jews living in villages throughout Germany became conscious of the hostility around them and tried to leave for the nearest city," said Ruth.

After being arrested on Kristallnacht, Ruth's brother Ernst was released first; he already had a visa for the

Storefronts of Jewish-owned businesses damaged during the Kristallnacht pogrom. Berlin, Germany, November 10, 1938.

United States and could prove he was leaving Germany. But it was several months before Ruth's father was let go. He'd been arrested three days before his sixtieth birthday and returned in the winter, ill and thin. One night soon after he came back, the family froze in fear when they heard a knock on the door. But this time was different. The local baroness had sent a servant with bread and a bottle of wine for Ruth's father.

Ruth's mother had been born in the city of Mannheim and had relatives there. She found work as the director of a boys' orphanage. Ruth's father could help out, and the family would have a place to live. The gift of bread and wine had been a small act of kindness, but it could not make up for everything else that had happened.

A destroyed business on the day after the November 1938 pogrom in Magdeburg, Germany.

Marianne
DON'T LET HIM COME HOME

"The ring at the door made my heart thump," remembered Marianne Elsley. "I opened the door; there stood two SS men in plain clothes."

The men demanded to see her father. Marianne explained that he was out. "They did not believe me and pushed their way in past me. They searched the flat very thoroughly, looking into cupboards and behind furniture, slowly and deliberately; it would have been quite pointless to hide. They tried under the beds and in the bath, he obviously was not there.

"When was he expected home? I didn't know. Where was he? I didn't know that either. This was true, but the answer was received with incredulity." The two men sat down to wait; they even lit a cigar belonging to Marianne's father.

"I stood there in terror praying inwardly, 'Please, God, don't let him come home, please, God, don't let him come home.' I knew quite well that the moment he appeared he would be arrested and marched off."

After the men left, Marianne ran outside, watching the street to warn her father. When he appeared, she told him what had happened. The family split up, staying with relatives and friends, leaving the apartment empty for a week. It worked for a while. Neighbors reported hearing SS men banging on the door in the middle of the night.

"In those days one was never sure of the system used for arrests. If a certain number was required for internment on a particular day, it sometimes paid off to hide out. If names appeared on the list it was pointless," said Marianne. "One of my uncles escaped arrest for several months by living in the Underground

Jewish men are arrested during Kristallnacht and forced to march through the town streets under SS guard to watch the desecration of a synagogue, then to be deported.

[subway]. He would travel back and forth on the various lines, day and night, and it is hard to imagine the anguish and boredom he suffered. His family would slip him food at pre-arranged stations. However, in the end, he could stand it no longer and he went home. But the SS evidently wanted him and had been looking for him. He was arrested almost at once and was never seen again."

What happened to Marianne's uncle, Lisa Seiden's father, and Ruth's father and brother was common. In addition to burning synagogues and looting private homes and stores, approximately thirty thousand prisoners were sent to concentration camps and held under horrible conditions for several months. While many men were released, historians estimate that more than a thousand died. The anonymity of a large city was no longer any protection against the Nazis. It was time to try to leave the country—if this could be done.

Newly arrived prisoners, still in their civilian clothes, and after shaving and disinfection, stand at roll call in Buchenwald concentration camp shortly after Kristallnacht.

Leslie

A WATERSHED

"Kristallnacht was a watershed for German and Austrian Jews," said Leslie Brent. "Those who had believed up to then that things must surely get better had their illusions rudely and dramatically shattered.

"The frantic scramble to emigrate began but by this time that had become extremely difficult. Not only were the German authorities unhelpful and required emigration payments, but most western countries had strict limitations on the issue of visas."

Leslie's family had moved to Berlin, where they tried to blend in with the population of a larger city. But they were struggling. "Having a relative or sponsor abroad and access to funds was undoubtedly a great help, but my parents, who like many others were by then totally impoverished, were left stranded."

∽

Kristallnacht was condemned by other nations. There were anti-Nazi demonstrations in New York. In response to news reports of the violence, President Franklin D. Roosevelt held a press conference soon after, on November 15, denouncing the actions.

Michael Creswell, head of the German Department of the British Foreign Office, stated, "'This far exceeds any other barbarities which the Nazis have been guilty of in the last five years. It is of quite a different order.'"

The Nazis weren't deterred by these condemnations. Far from it. The official newsletter of the SS carried an article speculating about possible reprisals for the harsh treatment of Jews. "'We shall take a thousand eyes for one eye, a thousand teeth for one tooth.'"

In fact, the Nazis took another lesson away from the international reaction. "Kristallnacht taught the Nazi administrators and planners that they must in future act with silence and secrecy, hiding what they were doing to the Jews from the eyes of world indignation. The less the outside world knew or saw, the more efficient would be whatever policy they chose, and the less liable to outside concern or interference."

The Nazis learned from the outcry. From this point on, their most heinous acts would be carried out mostly in secret.

$\backsim$

Between Hitler's assumption of power in January 1933 and the outbreak of war in September 1939, the official policy was to try to force Jews to emigrate. But it had become more and more difficult for families to leave Germany or Austria, even when they wanted desperately to do so. Immigration was subject to quotas, or limits, established by the United States and Great Britain, along with a host of other requirements.

One historian noted that "The United States took in by far the largest number during this period: almost 200,000 as a result of its long-established quota of 25,000 German immigrants a year. Britain took in the second largest number, more than 65,000 in the same six-year period. Between them Britain and the United States gave refuge to more than half of all German Jews living in Germany in January 1933."

And while there were approximately half a million Jews in Germany before the war, the number needing asylum expanded rapidly as Hitler moved to occupy and take control of other states in Europe. For example, when the Germans entered the city of Vienna on March 12, 1938, annexing Austria, approximately 183,000 more Jewish men, women, and children came under Nazi rule.

The attacks against Austrian Jews began almost immediately after the takeover, instilling fear and panic as families began searching for a way out, writing to relatives scattered in other places and trying desperately to get on waiting lists and obtain the proper paperwork, including travel visas, to leave. The word of the day was *visas*.

"'Visas! We began to live visas day and night,' remembered one immigrant. 'When we were awake, we were obsessed by visas. We talked about them all the time. Exit visas. Transit visas. Entrance visas. Where could we go? During the day, we tried to get the proper documents, approvals, stamps. At night, in bed, we tossed about and dreamed about long lines, officials, visas. Visas.'"

Where could we go? That was the question that haunted Jewish families. *And can we get out in time?*

Many people in the United States, England, and Australia were reluctant to take in more refugees. After the annexation of Austria, President Franklin D. Roosevelt requested an increase in the number of immigrants from Germany. But this went nowhere in the United States Congress; a chance to save more people was lost.

What about other countries? Could they step up efforts to help? Roosevelt tried to get more support by calling nations together. "On 6 July 1938 an international conference opened at Evian, on the shores of Lake Geneva, to discuss the future reception of refugees. By that time more than 250,000 Jews had already left Germany and Austria," noted historian Martin Gilbert. "The largest group, 155,000 by then, had been admitted to the United States. The British government had already admitted 40,000 and a further 8,000 into Palestine.

"France had taken in 15,000, whose fate would again hang in the balance within a few years, when France was defeated by Germany," wrote Gilbert. "Many were then to be saved a second time, in hiding, as a result of the courage of French men and women. Switzerland had taken in more than 14,000, who were to survive the war thanks to Swiss neutrality." But that left more than 300,000 German and Austrian Jews still seeking safety.

And while some Jews were hidden in France, others were betrayed to authorities. Recent scholars of the Holocaust have also examined the French government's role in retaining Jewish refugees in extremely poor conditions in internment camps, which, according to historians Debórah Dwork and Robert Jan van Pelt, "bulged with people who had fled to France to escape the Nazis. But when France fell, officials did not open the gates to give them a chance to escape. Worse: according to the armistice signed [with Germany] on 22 June [1940], the French betrayed the principle of asylum, agreeing to 'surrender upon demand all Germans named by the German Government in France as well as in French territories.'" In 1940, the Germans did not want the Jews. By the spring of 1942, Jews were being deported from French internment camps to Auschwitz.

∽

In the end, the 1938 conference on refugees in Evian was a failure. The world was not willing to step up.

"As the number of Jews attempting to leave grew, the restrictions against them also grew: Britain and the United States both tightened their rules for admission," wrote Gilbert. The historian noted that this trend could be seen in other nations as well. For example, Australia accepted only about fifteen hundred Jewish refugees. Some countries, such as Ireland, took none. Other nations, including Argentina, Chile, Uruguay, and Mexico, adopted laws that placed severe restrictions on the number of Jews admitted.

This was the complex reality facing the families of young people like Leslie Brent, Ruth David, and Marianne Elsley. England did not have a history of welcoming immigrants as the United States did and tightened its visa policies. The British government admitted only fifty Jewish doctors but did offer visas to more than ten thousand Jewish women who applied as domestic servants, since this was a need in Britain at the time.

With unemployment numbers still high in the United States because of the Great Depression, the country was unwilling to bring in refugees who might need public assistance. Claims of harassment or the need for asylum didn't matter.

In other words, as immigration historians Dwork and Van Pelt write, "With unemployment rampant in the United States throughout the 1930s, no one who depended upon finding a job on arrival was allowed entry. Another provision in the law prohibited everyone—except artists, ministers, professors, nurses, and domestic servants—to negotiate a job in advance." Some refugees were middle or upper class, and might have been able to bring money with them, but the Nazi government prohibited Jews from doing that.

$\sim$

IT ALL TOOK TIME

These restrictions meant that Jewish families had to deal with an all-but-impossible situation. The only option was to rely on friends and family in America to provide an affidavit, a document that testified they would be financially responsible for the immigrants. The process was slow and frustrating, and filled with many excruciating delays. As Marianne Elsley wrote later, "It all took time, too long, too long."

Marianne's father hadn't wanted to face the truth: The country he loved so deeply and served so well no longer wanted him. But after Kristallnacht, he and Marianne's mother tried desperately to leave. They applied for visas and contacted relatives. In addition to waiting in long lines and filling out paperwork, they started taking English language lessons to prepare them for life in another country.

Marianne dreaded it whenever her parents left the house for their evening language class. It wasn't that she was too young to stay home alone; she was simply petrified with worry. "I was left to pace up and down in the flat with a pounding heart, and peer out of the window, until I saw them come back. Then I would jump into bed and pretend to be asleep. No one will ever know how scared I was."

No wonder. Each day seemed to bring new anxieties. "Shop windows were smashed with monotonous regularity. One had to be extremely careful not to enter forbidden shops or cafes. A mistake would inevitably lead to arrest, and arrest was beginning to mean death."

After Kristallnacht, Ruth David's parents also focused more and more on *Auswanderung,* emigration. Her older brother Werner had already apprenticed himself to a farmer in preparation to emigrate to South America; Ernst had managed to get a visa for the United States. But what about the four younger children: Hannah, Ruth, Michael, and Feo?

For these families and so many others, the questions were endless: Would they be able to emigrate to England, America, Palestine, Shanghai, or South America? If they did go, how would they make a living? How could they learn a new language? How many refugees would these countries accept? What paperwork would be required and how long would it take?

Kristallnacht had struck like a warning bell, a sign that time was running out. But a lifeline was about to be thrown, at least for some.

THE JEWISH POPULATION IN EUROPE

According to the United States Holocaust Memorial Museum, most Jews in prewar Europe lived in Eastern Europe. "In 1933, approximately 9.5 million Jews lived in Europe, comprising 1.7% of the total European population. This number represented more than 60 percent of the world's Jewish population at that time, estimated at 15.3 million."

Around three million Jews, or 9 percent of the European Jewish population, lived in Poland; there were another two and a half million Jews in the European part of the Soviet Union. Other countries with Jewish populations included Romania, France, the Baltic nations, the Netherlands, and Belgium. Here are the breakdowns of other countries—Germany: 525,000; Hungary: 445,000; Czechoslovakia: 357,000; Austria: 200,000.

"During the ten months between Kristallnacht and the outbreak of war nearly as many German Jews left (120,000) as in the five and a half years before then (150,000)," wrote historian Martin Gilbert. "The Austrian emigration figures for the ten months were about 140,000. Thus more than a quarter of a million people left their homes and their homeland in the wake of that one night and day of violence."

Chapter Eight

HERE IS A CHANCE

"Wave after wave of refugees has drifted across the world, uprooted from their homes, penniless, destitute, no country found ready at hand to receive them, separated from their families and their surroundings," proclaimed Sir Samuel Hoare, the home secretary, speaking in Britain's House of Commons.

The date was November 21, 1938, less than two weeks from when reports of the Nazi violence of Kristallnacht shocked the world. The home secretary went on to describe a new initiative, a plan to help at least some Jewish children escape from the unknown dangers ahead under the Nazis. "Here is a chance of taking the young generation of a great people, here is a chance of mitigating to some extent the terrible sufferings of their parents and their friends."

And so Kindertransport was born. Refugee advocates and Jewish leaders in England had long wanted the British government to accept more immigrants from Germany. They'd catapulted into action just days after Kristallnacht, presenting a plan to Prime Minister Neville Chamberlain on the evening of November 15. They promised to step up support so newcomers wouldn't be a drain on public funds. (Like the United States, the British government required anyone entering the country to prove they could support themselves.)

While that initial meeting had limited success, the home secretary had lent his support to the idea. A week later he proposed the effort to rescue Jewish children. In the end, about ten thousand children would be part of the program. A similar initiative in the United States failed to get support in Congress.

Some key elements made Kindertransport successful: The Home Office simplified entry procedures into Great Britain for unaccompanied children up to age seventeen. Children wouldn't need visas like normal travelers; nor would they need the usual travel documents issued by the German government. Instead, each child would have a simple identity card that would serve as a travel permit.

And, finally, for Kindertransport to work, concerned, loving parents had to make the heart-wrenching decision to part with their children and send them alone to a foreign country to be cared for by strangers, including those who might not share their own religious beliefs or traditions.

A coalition of refugee groups and religious (including Jewish and Quaker) groups, eventually called the Refugee Children's Movement, came together to work on arrangements. Appeals for foster families were placed in newspapers; holiday camps on the southern coast of England were rented as temporary housing; an office was rented.

From the beginning, the office was deluged with inquiries from anxious Jewish parents. "Even before its life-saving operation could begin, a vast, hastily assembled and inexperienced staff, composed mostly of volunteers, was besieged by heart-rending appeals for help from parents in Austria and Germany and frantic relatives already in Britain."

Refugee worker Norman Bentwich traveled to Amsterdam to work out details, since trains would pass through Holland. Arrangements were made to ferry the children across the North Sea on the last leg of their journey, with ferries departing from the Hook of Holland. Word went out to Jewish organizations in Germany detailing the effort and asking for help

The passport issued to a girl named Eva Rosenbaum a few days before
she left on a Kindertransport to England.

in selecting children and arranging their travel. It would be too difficult to select the children from afar: that would have to take place on the ground in Germany and Austria.

Although no one then could anticipate the ultimate horror of the Holocaust or the exact date when Hitler's aggressive military vision might trigger war, everyone seemed to share the feeling that time was running out.

A JOB TO BE DONE

Norbert Wollheim was committed to the Jewish community in Berlin. After Kristallnacht, he worked to help traumatized families, providing meals and support. He was twenty-five years old and had recently married. He and his wife, Rosa, hoped to start a family. They were also working hard to make arrangements to leave Germany.

One day, a fellow volunteer took Norbert aside and told him, "'Listen, I just got a call . . . and there's a job to be done. I understand that the British are willing to take children.'"

Norbert was urged to go see Otto Hirsch, executive director of a Jewish welfare organization called the Reichsvertretung, or Reich Representation of German Jews. Its core mission was to help Jews deal with the ever-tightening laws of the Nazis. Hirsch and others assisted families preparing to emigrate. They also helped Jews who'd lost their jobs and were struggling to survive.

Hirsch asked Norbert, who had been involved with Jewish youth groups, to help with the children's rescue effort. Norbert agreed but also shared that he was in the middle of efforts to leave the country. Hirsch assured him, "'I can give you my promise that when this will be done . . . it will be our commitment and our obligation to help you and your family to get out of Germany.'"

Like Jewish spiritual leader Rabbi Leo Baeck, Otto Hirsch himself refused to leave Germany and the people he served. For a while, these two men were protected by their positions and international contacts. Eventually, Rabbi Baeck was sent to Theresienstadt concentration camp, where he survived. After the war, he became the first president of the Leo Baeck Institute, which was founded to preserve the legacy of German-speaking Jews. (Some of the stories of Kindertransport survivors in this book are part of its collection.)

But Otto Hirsch could not fulfill his promise to help Norbert and his family. Hirsch was arrested. Despite efforts to secure his release, he was sent to Mauthausen concentration camp, where he died in June 1941. Today there is a bridge in Stuttgart, Germany, named in his memory.

In late November 1938, Norbert Wollheim got his first look at the Berlin office that would become the center of rescue operations for the Kindertransport. His stomach dropped when he saw the disorganized mess awaiting him. "There was a big conference room . . . covered with cards, heaps of cards and there was a desk which was covered with papers and the telephone was constantly ringing."

Norbert went right to work. He called friends he knew from the Jewish youth movement to come in and help. They quickly developed a system to accept applications from families and match children with the cards (which were entry permits). Norbert also took charge of organizing the transports. Children's lives were at stake, so he paid careful attention to every small detail. He made sure there were copies of passenger lists for the German authorities and for London too, so arrangements could be made to meet the children and place them with foster families. And, of course, Norbert fielded many calls from desperate parents who wanted to help their children escape even if they could not.

Norbert and others also would serve as escorts and accompany the transports. Norbert arranged for special permission letters to be issued to protect the escorts' safety. That way, he and others could go to London and return, and not be arrested by the German authorities.

Setting up a complicated rescue system like this so quickly wasn't easy. It was all done without computers, email, or fax machines. Even international phone communication could be difficult at times. But perhaps the hardest task Norbert faced didn't have anything to do with logistics. He had to speak to the parents saying goodbye to their children.

Norbert remembered giving last-minute instructions to families in a room or waiting area of the train station. "When the hour of departure came closer, I ascended a chair," Norbert recalled. He addressed the parents. "'Ladies and gentlemen, the time has arrived to say goodbye, because we are under strict orders not to let you accompany your children to the platform. The escorts will take over . . . but you cannot come. Please cooperate and don't make our work more difficult.'"

Years later, Norbert reflected on those moments, "I still admire these people, how courageous they were. Nobody broke down, but also there was the expectation that sooner or later they would be reunited again. . . .

"And I also must say that at this time nobody could have thought for a moment that this would for many, for almost ninety percent, be the last goodbye. Nobody could expect that a year and a half later after these transports had rolled to the west into freedom, that transports would leave for the east into the slaughterhouses of Hitler in Auschwitz or Treblinka."

And so, on December 1, 1938, the first children on the Kindertransport gathered at the train station in Berlin. Leslie Brent was one of them.

Part Three

FLIGHT

1938–1939

My parents' unspoken decision was to get the children out. Whatever else had to be done, that was the first and most important thing.

—FREDERIC ZELLER

I remember dreaming that no matter what you did they could always find you.

—THEA FELIKS EDEN

Beate Siegel (right) and two other girls look out a train window as they leave Germany on a Kindertransport to England.

TO WANDER

Auswanderung: emigration. In German the word is vivid, less abstract than in English. *Aus*; "out"; *wandern*: "to wander". When I was a young child this word was part of our daily vocabulary for as long as I can remember. The word frightened me. Where would we go? How would we wander? Like pilgrims? Like beggars? . . .

Why emigrate? Decades later I know more than ever that no one emigrates happily or easily. The decision to leave for the unknown, especially for parents with family responsibilities, is horrendously difficult. . . . An emigrant, who is barred from returning, is a homeless refugee.

—RUTH DAVID

Chapter Nine

INTO THE UNKNOWN

Leslie

MY LIFE WAS SAVED

In late summer, Leslie Brent's orphanage had been stormed by a mob. Leslie and his friend had hidden in a dark corner under the rafters. The orphanage was spared on Kristallnacht itself, though another children's home in Berlin was totally destroyed. When the director of Leslie's orphanage heard about Kindertransport, he nominated several boys to leave on the first transport.

And so, on December 1, Leslie found himself at the train station in Berlin along with about two hundred other children, many from the other orphanage that had been attacked, and eight leaders. Leslie couldn't recall too many details of this chaotic scene. His parents did their best to hide their emotions. He had some sandwiches for the journey.

It was tense as they pulled out of the station. "The train was patrolled by German police and we had been warned to be on our best behavior and not to make any noise," Leslie recalled. "And so we rattled through the German countryside, stopping occasionally. Whenever the train stopped there was a marked rise in the tension, for fear that we would be ordered to leave."

Everyone relaxed when they crossed the border into Holland. "Even so, my facial expression in the photograph taken of the children in my compartment . . . is distinctly wistful; the face of a child who had no inkling what the future held."

The group boarded a ship named the *De Praag* for the crossing, and arrived in Harwich at five thirty in the morning on Friday, December 2. Leslie's new life was about to begin.

Members of the first Kindertransport. Leslie Brent is standing third from left in the back (to the left of the boy in the glasses).

Marianne
A WARM WINTER COAT

After Kristallnacht, Marianne Elsley's parents kept trying to find a way to emigrate, taking English classes and contacting relatives in other countries. But they determined to send fifteen-year-old Marianne to safety first. As an only child, Marianne was especially close to her parents.

"When my father heard that I was to leave, he cried—not with relief, but at the thought of losing his only child, whom he feared he would never see again. How right he was! My mother and I cried together too, we were devoted to each other, and separation was going to be hard. Fortunately, I did not then know how bitter and agonizing homesickness can be, or I should have refused to go."

Instead, Marianne was swept up in preparations. Her mother scraped together some clothes for Marianne. She gave Marianne her own best dress and made two new blouses and a skirt.

"I absolutely hated leaving them, for although at that time there was no immediate thought of war, I felt it was forever. I am sure that they had the same feeling. We sat together for hours, talking, my parents advising me to be good, and grateful and helpful and tidy, and assuring me how lucky I was."

Then, on a cold morning in January 1939, Marianne

found herself at the train station in Berlin. The moment of parting had come.

Members of the first Kindertransport arrive in Harwich, England.

Ruth
I WAVED TILL I COULD
NO LONGER SEE THEM

After Kristallnacht and the attack on their home, Ruth David's family had moved to the larger city of Mannheim. Ruth's mother found a job as the director of a boys' orphanage, where her family could also live. They hoped things would be better away from the village, where everyone except their friend and former housekeeper, Mina Dümig, had turned against them.

Ruth's elderly uncle Gustav and his sister, Ida, stayed

behind. Ruth never saw them again. She learned later that her aunt Ida was murdered at Auschwitz. Uncle Gustav died three weeks after being deported to Theresienstadt concentration camp.

In Mannheim, nine-year-old Ruth ventured outside only when she was with others. "We had learned that we must make ourselves as invisible as possible." At least no one threw stones at them or shouted insults.

By now, Ruth's two older half brothers had left: Werner to Argentina and Ernst to the United States. "My parents must have heard about the Kindertransport and put my sister's and my name down for the emigration scheme. They did not tell us. Nearer the time for departure they discovered that through some muddle Hannah and I could not leave together and I would have to go first. They told me only a few days before I was due to depart."

Ruth felt dismayed. She cried and hated that she had to go alone. She barely knew where England was on the map. "I had experienced enough to know that life was not going to improve for us, that we were in real danger," she said.

But to go alone and be separated from her family was frightening. Ruth had only a week to get ready. "I was exhausted by the speed of events, the positive encouragement, the packing. What little time I had on my own I spent looking despairingly into the vacant, unknown future, hoping above all that this banishment would be short."

The night before Ruth's departure on June 6, 1939, her parents laid their hands on her head and blessed her. "The goodbyes were not tearful, Mother insisted that we would soon be reunited, and I waved to them until I could no longer see them. I did wonder whether this was the last time, and tried to chase the thought away."

Ruth remembered little of the train journey itself. In Holland, some Dutch ladies brought drinks and oranges. The children were taken onto a ship for the crossing. "It was dark when we reached the ferry at Hook van Holland and I tried to be excited about being on a ship for the first time in my life. But it didn't work. I broke into sobs."

Ruth's new life—alone and apart from everyone she knew and loved—was about to begin.

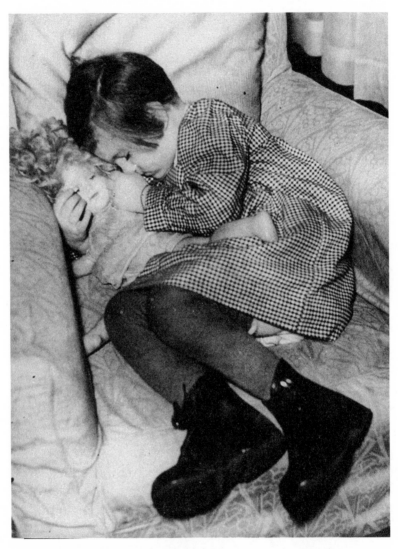

A close-up of a little girl sleeping with her doll in a chair. She was one of the newly arrived refugee children of the second Kindertransport, December 12, 1938.

PARTING

IT WAS VERY COLD

"One day, quite unprepared for what was about to happen, I found myself at the main station in Vienna. There were a lot of people, lots of children, lots of noise," said Lisa Leist Seiden. "I had my doll with me and as it was very cold, I had dressed her up in her best outfit. A woolen coat, a cap with earmuffs, mittens, and long white stockings."

It was December 17, 1938, and Lisa was nine. The station was busy and noisy. Lisa's mother led her to a quiet corner and hoisted her up so they could talk face-to-face. "'I want you to listen to me very, very carefully. It is very important that you understand what I am going to tell you,'" her mother said.

Her mother's voice was so urgent, Lisa listened carefully. "'It is necessary for us to part for some time, but I want you and Peter to stay together, come what may.'" She made Lisa promise again and again.

Years later, Lisa wondered why she had no memory of seeing her mother's face as the train pulled out. She finally realized it was because her mother wasn't allowed on the platform. The children were gathered in a large hall where goodbyes were said. Then the escorts led the children to the train, leaving their parents behind. (This procedure seems to have been followed in most of the transports with large groups. However, in some cases, individual children began the journey from small stations; others do recall saying goodbye to their families on the platform.)

A young girl on a Kindertransport.

DID IT MAKE IT EASIER FOR THEM?

Bernd Koschland was born in a town near Nuremberg, Germany, in 1931. On Kristallnacht, his father was taken to Dachau. "Today on the wall of my study is a copy of a photograph of him standing in line with other prisoners." Shortly after, his parents decided to send him to England. His sister would follow.

"I will never understand how my parents must have felt when they made the decision to send the two of us away. The 'promise' that they would soon join us no doubt eased our way; but did it make it easier for them?" said Bernd.

"How did I feel? I cannot recall . . . All I can guess is that I must have been very upset; I would miss my parents, but I believed that they would join me soon."

That was not to be.

CLOSE CALLS

Berlin-based Kindertransport rescuer Norbert Wollheim sometimes accompanied the transports. There were strict rules that nothing of value was allowed to cross the border; each child could bring just a small amount of money.

Once in Harwich, England, the ferries' destination, Norbert heard his name called. A customs official was questioning a boy who had a violin. Was it the boy's instrument, or simply a way to smuggle a costly object out of Germany?

Norbert suggested to the official that the boy be allowed to play. All the time he was in a cold sweat: Could the boy play the instrument, or was this simply a way to get around the rules and keep something valuable out of the hands of the Nazis, who'd already forced Jewish families to hand over precious jewelry and silverware?

Norbert asked the boy to play, then held his breath. A hush fell on everyone as the first strains of music filled the room. He could play! In fact, he was playing

A boy with a violin on a Kindertransport.

the British anthem, "God Save the King," as a tribute to the country willing to give him refuge.

The customs official waved them through.

Norbert also recalled a situation even more serious. During one ferry crossing, he and other escorts discovered a serious mistake: one of the children was eighteen, over the age limit of seventeen for Kindertransport refugees.

Norbert couldn't believe they'd gotten this far without being caught. "The boy had already gone to sleep, and when they brought him down, I almost fainted."

The reason? Norbert saw that the boy's head was shaven; he realized what that meant. The boy must have been arrested and put into a concentration camp after Kristallnacht. He'd been released, probably under orders to leave Germany. Norbert and his team huddled, trying to decide what to do. This could be the young man's only chance to escape. They decided their only option was to lie: If asked, the boy should say he was seventeen and that his paperwork was wrong.

As he feared, Norbert was soon summoned by the immigration officer. The officer said that since the boy was already eighteen, he couldn't be admitted into England.

Norbert did the only thing he could: He bluffed, saying there must be some mistake in the paperwork and the boy was actually only seventeen. He called the boy, who by now was shaking with fear. The immigration officer took in the situation.

Then he asked Norbert, "'Do you take it as your responsibility to say that this is a mistake?'

"'Yes, sir, I do.'

"And there was a long time of silence. And I realized that he knew I was lying, and I knew that he knew that I was lying," said Norbert. "And he looked at the boy again . . . and after a moment of life and death for that boy, he took out the stamp, 'Admitted to United Kingdom.'"

Years later, reflecting on that moment, Norbert said, "Probably this man is not around anymore, but he has earned his place in heaven."

A GREAT ADVENTURE

When their parents told Frieda Korobkin and her three siblings they were leaving Vienna on a special Kindertransport for the children of Orthodox Jews, they tried to make the journey seem exciting. "We are told that we are embarking on a great adventure, first by train and then by boat," Frieda wrote later. Frieda had only ever ridden in a tramcar before, so, at the beginning at least, she felt excited. The six-year-old wouldn't be alone either. Her eleven-year-old sister, Mimi, would watch over her.

Frieda's last memory of home was seeing her mother and grandmother, sobbing in each other's arms. It was a cold walk to the train station. Her father, a devout rabbinical scholar, held tight to her mittened hands; her mittens were attached together by a cord around her neck so she wouldn't lose them. Frieda noticed Christmas decorations and bright lights on the street. Even more prevalent were the large posters and the Nazi flags.

What Frieda didn't notice were the two thugs in brown shirts and black boots. They threw her father up against a wall and then, with a flash of steel, cut off his beard. When the attack was over her father was silent. His lip was bleeding. He took Frieda's hand again and they kept on as before.

The scene at the station remained vivid in Frieda's mind's eye. "Parents and children clung and tore at each other and gazed into each other's eyes for what they knew might be the last time, desperately trying to store each feature in their memory banks. Above the harsh clackety-clack of locomotives arriving and departing, above the train whistles, above the shrieking of brakes and hissing of steam, there rose wave after wave of anguish that formed itself into a primeval wail that had no beginning and no end. Like some monstrous, mortally wounded beast in its final throes of agony.

"Was it at that moment that it dawned on me that perhaps this might not be such a wonderful adventure after all? Is that why, when the time came to board the train, my father had to force me kicking and screaming into the carriage?

"I was so angry with him that I refused to look at him again or wave goodbye from the train window, despite Mimi's urging. As a result, I am haunted forever by the image of my father standing desolate and bleeding on that station platform, watching helplessly as the train carrying his four children vanished before his eyes."

In Holland, Frieda met Rabbi Solomon Schonfeld. Schonfeld has been credited with arranging the rescue of a thousand or more Orthodox Jewish children, including Frieda and her siblings. A tall man, he seemed like a giant to Frieda. He leaned over and teased her, wondering if such a small girl could speak Yiddish (a language used by Central and Eastern European Jews).

And, of course, she could. What Frieda couldn't know was that someday she would have a son who would follow in the devout footsteps of Rabbi Schonfeld and the grandfather he never met. Today, Rabbi Daniel

Korobkin serves the Beth Avraham Yoseph community of Toronto, Canada.

GO FORWARD AND DON'T LOOK BACK

On June 20, 1939, a few months after his tenth birthday, Freddie Traum left Vienna on a Kindertransport along with his sister, Ruth. A few days before, his father took a family photo. "We all went downstairs to the backyard where my father set up the tripod and camera, placed a black cloth over his head, and focused the camera on us to take our picture. He selected the delayed shutter feature and joined us in the photograph.

"Our mother was taking us to the West Bahnhof, the railroad station for trains heading west. As we were about to leave, my father said to me, 'Go forward and don't look back.' I was never quite sure of what he meant by that statement, but I believe it to have been more philosophical in nature than in the literal manner a small child would take it. However, as the three of us proceeded along the sidewalk but were still a short distance from our home, I did stop and turn around to look back, and just as I expected my father was at the bay window with tears in his eyes, forcing a smile, watching us walk out of his life."

I CAN'T SPEAK ENGLISH

John Fieldsend's family had moved to Czechoslovakia, where they hoped to be safer. But the Nazis had marched in there too, as part of Hitler's relentless plan for expansion.

One day, his father told John that both he and his brother, Arthur, would be leaving. "'I have something very important to tell you. You are going on a long journey. You are to travel to a country called England. You will have to go alone; we can't come with you. Maybe one day, when the present troubles are over, you will be able to return, or maybe we can join you, but for now you will have to go alone.'"

John's father taught him to say, "I can't speak English." His mother snapped a photograph of John and Arthur, along with their father and the family dog. At the train station a few days later, John's mother gave him her wristwatch as a keepsake.

Before going to England, the boys were first sent to a boarding school in Hanover, Germany. After some weeks there (John couldn't recall how long), they were put on a train with other children and some adults.

"We travelled on through Germany in a silent mood of fear as there were also some Nazi guards on board. We then came to an international border, which turned out to be with Holland. The Nazi guards got off, some much more friendly adults got on and we travelled on to a place where we got onto a boat. By then it was dark and we were tired so I have only blurred memories."

When they reached Holland, the children were moved onto a ship for the rough sea crossing. The boat docked in the seaside town of Harwich, England. From there, the children boarded a train for Liverpool Street in London, where they were met by host families and volunteers.

"The station platform was alive with hundreds of children with labels round our necks, jabbering away in Czech and German. There were groups of adults not understanding a word and looking at the labels for particular names and numbers, and there were a few organizers trying to keep some sense of order."

One night in 1988, fifty years later, John's 1938 travel permit photo appeared on a British television program. That was the first time he realized he was among 669 children rescued through the efforts of a group of dedicated rescuers, including a young stockbroker named Nicholas Winton. Winton became involved when, instead of going on a planned ski holiday in Switzerland, he visited a friend who was assisting refugees in Prague.

Winton plunged into the work. With support from the London-based Movement for the Care of Children from Germany, and dedicated workers in Prague, including unsung heroes like Trevor Chadwick, Doreen Warriner, and Beatrice Wellington, the group began with airlifts, but after March 1939, when the Germans marched into Prague, most rescues were by train.

Chadwick often had to cajole the Nazi authorities to give permission for the children to travel, and the rescue operation wasn't always done by the book. "When essential papers had failed to come through to Prague, Chadwick had decided to cut corners by manufacturing a few of his own," wrote one historian. "Convincing enough to persuade the Germans that London had kept to the bureaucratic niceties, the stamp of approval was secured and away went the train."

Rescuer Nicholas Winton holds a boy who was
being flown from Prague to London in
January 1939.

LOOK, LISTEN, REMEMBER: In 2003, rescuer
Nicholas Winton (1909–2015) was knighted by Queen
Elizabeth II for his efforts. Following the war, Sir Winton
didn't speak much about his rescue work, which
remained mostly unknown until 1988, when his wife
happened upon a scrapbook he kept with the names
and photos of children, including John Fieldsend.
Efforts continue to recognize other rescuers in
Czechoslovakia, including Trevor Chadwick, Doreen
Warriner, and Marie Schmolka.

To learn more, watch the film *Children Saved from the Nazis: The Story of Sir Nicholas Winton*: https://www.youtube.com/watch?v=nT0yPjj0UqQ. Read more about Sir Winton at USHMM: https://encyclopedia.ushmm.org/content/en/article/nicholas-winton-and-the-rescue-of-children-from-czechoslovakia-1938-1939.

To find out more about Trevor Chadwick, visit: https://www.theguardian.com/world/2015/jul/03/forgotten-heroes-of-the-kindertransports. To learn about Marie Schmolka's work with refugees and children, visit: https://marieschmolka.org/about-marie-schmolka/ and http://www.thejc.com/news/uk-news/marking-the-life-of-a-forgotten-heroine-1.445765.

Chapter Ten

FRED'S PASSPORT

LAST BLESSING

"From time to time, when things look dark and life presents problems . . . I reach into my desk drawer and pull out a German passport, which was issued to me in 1938," said Fred Rosenbaum. "On the cover of this document, prominently displayed is a German eagle with a swastika in its claws. When you open the passport, a rubber-stamped 'J' in red ink is the first thing that you see to indicate that I am Jewish. The passport was issued to Fritz Rosenbaum, which was my name before I became a citizen of the United States."

Fred's passport held a lot of memories. He could remember his mother's ordeal trying to get it for him.

"As people would assemble at night, standing in line for hours to obtain these precious passports, truckloads of storm troopers would descend upon those waiting in line."

Fred Rosenbaum was born in 1926 in Vienna, Austria, and was about twelve when Kristallnacht took place. He'd managed to escape Hitler Youth at his school that November day. Soon after, his parents got word of children's transports leaving Vienna, and they managed to get Fred a place. "My mother packed my suitcase (small as it was), and I made my last visit to my grandparents who were destined to stay in Vienna and subsequently be killed in one of Hitler's concentration camps.

"I remember so clearly my grandfather placing his hands on my head and giving me his last blessing and saying, 'Fritz, the dear Lord will take care of you.'

"My mother took me to the railroad station where all the children were assembled and checked off the roster. A cardboard tag was tied around my neck with my name, birth date, destination, and the name of the family who was going to pick me up at the railroad station in London."

After a tearful goodbye, Fred sat on the train. SS troops came on board, searching for anything valuable the children might be carrying, like watches or jewelry. Fred felt relieved when they left and the train chugged along to the border. "At the first stop in Holland, we were greeted by Dutch ladies who brought hot chocolate, sandwiches, and cakes on board to feed us."

The next day found Fred in London, standing on the platform waiting for someone to collect him. One by one, the other children left as those who'd signed up to foster the young refugees stepped forward. But no one came for Fred.

"Finally I was the only child left on the platform of the railroad station. No one had arrived to take care of me. One of the staff people in charge of the transport took me home with her for the night. It was a most uncomfortable situation as I spoke hardly any English, with the exception of hello, goodbye, and thank you.

"My clothing was different from that worn by school children my age in London. I was extremely lonely, scared, and totally confused. But the next morning, the family that was supposed to pick me up at the railroad station arrived by taxi, most apologetic. They had set the wrong day on the calendar. They picked me up and took me to their home in the east end of London. . . .

"They gave me a small bedroom where I hung up my few clothes, sat on the bed, and cried in that absolute loneliness only a child can know who has been separated from everyone and everything he loved, not knowing what the future would bring."

Fred started school. At first, he was put in with a

first grade class, which was humiliating for a twelve-year-old. School was hard, and so was Fred's foster home. Although he started with a room of his own, that didn't last. He was forced to share a room and even a bed with the grandfather of the family. "I was confronted with a total lack of privacy, at home, in school and in the strange city; my loneliness and depression and my desperate need for my parents, who were I knew not where, became almost unbearable."

Luckily for Fred, a visit by someone in charge of the child refugees resulted in his being placed with a different foster family. Once more, Fred packed his small suitcase and had to face a new family and school. That situation didn't last either, and Fred was eventually moved to a boarding school.

Unlike most of the Kindertransport refugees, Fred's story took a miraculous turn. His parents were able to get to England. The family obtained affidavits for the United States, where they arrived in 1941. They lived first in Washington State, and then moved to Portland, Oregon. At age eighteen, Fred joined the United States Army. After the war, he earned a bachelor's degree from Portland State University and began a successful career in business.

Years later, watching his own grandchildren, Fred wrote, "I look at them and thank God that they do not have to experience what I did at their age. I think of those desperate times and wonder how so many of us survived our separation from our parents, loved ones, and homeland. Yet I know that other children faced far worse situations."

Fred Rosenbaum rose to the rank of brigadier general in the Oregon Air National Guard and received numerous awards for his humanitarian actions and community service. He never forgot his own experiences and founded a summer camp for children. Upon Fred's death in 2010, at age eighty-three, Oregon's governor said, "'Oregon is less of a place because Fred has died. . . .'

"'Anybody who got to know Dad understood his experience in Nazi Germany impacted his entire life,' said Fred's son, Mark. 'All of his work stemmed from an extreme appreciation for the freedom and opportunity presented by this country and his understanding of what it was like to be dis-

A numbered identification tag worn by Henry Schmelzer when he was on a Kindertransport from Austria to England in December 1938.

criminated against based on religion and the impact of economic deprivation.'"

Chapter Eleven

THEA'S NARROW ESCAPE

Thea Feliks Eden didn't board a train from her home or from a temporary stay in a Jewish orphanage. Instead, she escaped after long months in the Zbaszyn internment camp on the Polish border. Thea almost didn't make it out: She was on one of the last transports before World War II erupted on September 1, 1939.

Thea hailed from Cologne, Germany; her father died when she was six, and her mother was originally from Poland. To Thea, who was born in 1926, it seemed as though the Nazis were "always there." She grew up feeling threatened as she walked to school; she got used to seeing signs in store windows declaring that Jews weren't welcome.

Once, when Thea was standing in front of her own house, a child threw a rock and hit her. Thea felt blood streaming down her face. The stone had missed her eye by a fraction of an inch. Thea soon learned not to speak to anyone, in a world that seemed, every day, ever more "dangerous, crazy, and evil."

Thea's mother had been born in Poland. In October 1938, the Polish government declared Thea's mother's passport invalid. Shortly before Kristallnacht, along with thousands of others, Thea's family was rounded up and taken away.

"A day you get up—it's like any other day. Suddenly there are Nazis at the door, and they tell you you're leaving your home, right now. You pack your suitcase and you've got to be at the station at five o'clock, or else," said Thea.

Thea and her family were part of the group of more than twelve thousand Jews of Polish descent expelled by Germany. With their Polish passports invalidated, they'd become stateless. The families were taken by train or in vans across the border, where the refugees were housed in abandoned buildings near the town of Zbaszyn, Poland.

As we've already seen, this event had wide repercussions. One family deported from Hanover was the

Before escaping on a Kindertransport in August 1939, Thea Feliks Eden was one of thousands of refugees living in horrific conditions in Zbaszyn on the border of Germany and Poland.

Grynszpans, whose son, Herschel, was living in Paris. His subsequent killing of a German official was used by the Nazis as the rationale for Kristallnacht.

$\sim$

When the train carrying Thea's family and the others stopped, Thea saw nothing but an old, broken-down mill and abandoned horse stalls. This is where the refugees had to stay—and the conditions were appalling.

"Zbaszyn is on the border between Germany and Poland. Well, you should have seen what we had in that camp. These were empty, dilapidated buildings that were considered unfit for human habitation," said Thea. "The outhouses were holes in the ground. You looked down there and there were rats. And that was the place where you had to go, because there wasn't any other place to go. . . . You look down and you see beady rat eyes."

Thea spent ten months in the camp. Although someone tried to set up some teaching for the children, mostly kids were left to roam. "There was nothing for us to do. There was no place for us to go."

Thea watched women give birth; she saw an old woman die. Without access to water, it was impossible to keep clean, and people got sick. "You were basically dirty, very, very dirty," Thea remembered.

One of the worst things was the lice, which were so

bad Thea carried scars from their bites the rest of her life. She recalled that she and the other children had to act like monkeys, grooming one another and picking lice eggs out of their hair. It didn't really work. She called it "the agony of lice."

Before being deported to Zbaszyn, Thea's mother had been trying to get her children onto any rescue list she could. And she kept trying. Thea was never sure exactly how her mother did it, but she managed to save her three eldest children. "The fact that she got three of us out, three out of four of the children is a tribute to her tenacity, her ingenuity, self-sacrifice . . . and sheer guts," Thea said years later. "I saw my mother the last time, oddly enough, on my birthday, my thirteenth birthday [August 25, 1939]."

Thea barely made it out of Poland. The train was heading to the Polish port of Gdynia, on the Baltic Sea. "We were actually on the last ship that left Gdynia. . . . By the time we got to England war had broken out. . . . A week later it wouldn't have happened," Thea recalled. "It would have been too late."

In England, Thea was placed with several different families, all of them Christian. She had no adults to support her Jewish faith. She went to school with refugees as well as English children who'd been evacuated from London to the countryside for fear of bombing raids on the city (the Blitz).

Thea learned to detach her head from her heart. She learned to function—at least on the outside. "But there was also this hurt child who you never talked about, kept hidden," she said. "I don't think those things ever heal. How could they heal, if it's never dealt with? It's a buried thing. It's just like an ache, or a pain, or a sore that doesn't go away, but that you accept.

"I think a lot of tears were shed in silence, under blankets."

A RESCUER'S STORY

Norbert Wollheim helped rescue seven thousand children on the Kindertransport. Each time he made a trip to London as an escort, he returned to Germany, just as he'd promised the Germans he would do. It wasn't just to please the authorities: His wife and, eventually, his little son were still there. Plus, he felt if he didn't return he might endanger the entire Kindertransport rescue operation.

Norbert was supposed to accompany a transport in September 1939. War clouds were looming, and so the date was changed to August 29. Norbert decided not to go. Had he been on it, he might have been in England when war broke out.

Norbert's dedication to the children on the Kindertransport extracted a terrible price. In the spring of 1943, Norbert, along with his wife and young son, were deported to the Auschwitz death camp. His parents and sister were also arrested and taken from their home.

On their arrival at Auschwitz after a harrowing train ride, Norbert was separated from his family. He never saw his wife and child again. His parents and sister were also killed. Norbert was the only one to survive.

Later, Norbert said that his survival was partly a matter of luck. Norbert had been trained as a welder. He was put to work in an offshoot labor camp of Auschwitz called Buna/Monowitz. He was assigned to a skilled metalworker group and made to do slave labor for a company. It was I.G. Farben, the same company where Edith Rosenthal Lavender had once been a typist.

Late in the war, in 1945, the German Army was on the run from Russian and American troops. Norbert became part of a death march of prisoners being driven through Germany. The prisoners were kept under guard. One night the men in Norbert's group were caught in the woods, with Russian troops behind them, and Allies up ahead. In the confusion, Norbert and a friend managed to escape from their captors and evade being shot.

When they reached the nearest road, Norbert and his friend discovered it was crowded with the remnants of the German Army and refugees escaping Berlin in whatever vehicle they could get their hands on: milk vans, fire trucks, cars, even hearses. If their vehicle ran out of gas, people simply abandoned it and walked slowly along.

Norbert and his friend decided their best bet was to try to blend in with the other civilians. Luckily, Norbert had thrown away the striped coat that marked him as a prisoner.

They walked and walked—all night long. Norbert was so exhausted and malnourished he felt as if he was dozing as he shuffled. Suddenly, toward dawn, his friend cried, "'Norbert, isn't that the American flag?'"

Sure enough, it was. "When we saw that . . . we were laughing and we were crying. [We] embraced each other and it was unreal, because it was a feeling of being born again. When you are born you don't know about it because you have no recollection, but this moment of rebirth is something . . . it's very special. I think you cannot describe it properly. The human language is too poor to do that."

They soon spotted an American officer. As they approached, the soldier pointed his pistol at them. Norbert had a little English, enough to explain that they were prisoners of the camps. The American gave them food; Norbert ate sparingly. He realized stuffing himself could be dangerous since he was so severely malnourished.

Norbert was safe, at last. But he was alone: His wife and child had been sent to the gas chambers immediately upon arriving at Auschwitz.

Norbert rebuilt his life after the war; he remarried and had two children. He became a tireless advocate for commemoration of victims of the Holocaust. In 1950, Norbert sued for compensation for his forced slave labor at I.G. Farben, which resulted in a global settlement to compensate him and other survivors. In 1951, Norbert and his family moved to the United States, where he worked as an accountant. Today, there is a memorial to Norbert located on the former site of the I.G. Farben company headquarters that educates visitors on the Holocaust.

Before his death in New York in 1998 at the age of eighty-five, Norbert recorded his personal story, including his work organizing Kindertransport rescues, for the United States Holocaust Memorial Museum in Washington, DC.

LOOK, LISTEN, REMEMBER: Visit the USHMM online to watch and listen to Norbert describe his harrowing experience of forced labor: https://encyclopedia.ushmm.org/content/en/oral-history/norbert-wollheim-describes-forced-labor-at-the-buna-works-1.

Part Four

SEPARATION AND SORROW

1939 and Beyond

You can't chase away darkness with a broom. You have to chase away darkness with light.

—RABBI YOSEF ITKIN,
OCTOBER 28, 2018

Goodness, kindness, love, honesty, decency: those are the standard ethics. I mean, I didn't invent them. But if people lived . . . an ethical life there would be none of this business happening in the world today.

—SIR NICHOLAS WINTON

German troops parade through Warsaw, Poland, in September 1939.

From that last journey, I remember only smells.

The noise of the train has been buried in my memory, as have the faces of other passengers, their voices and the content of their conversations.

I've forgotten what I thought about as I left the land of my childhood, leaving behind my parents and all my memories.

All I remember is the smell of sea spray when the train drew into the Hook of Holland.

I'm now ninety-two years old and I can smell it still.

It was nighttime.

I heard the murmur of waves mingling with the sound of the wind.

We boarded a liner. In the dark of night it was still impossible to make out the sea that I so desperately wanted to see. It finally appeared at dawn.

And, for the first time, I saw the horizon.

—EDGAR FEUCHTWANGER

LIFE IN A STRANGE LAND

A BOILED ONION

Thea Feliks Eden's first days in England were full of strange sights and new experiences. She'd survived months of horrific conditions in a camp on the German-Polish border and barely made it out of Europe before war put an end to rescue transports. She missed her mother and siblings.

For the first couple of days in London, Thea and the other children were housed in a hotel, with soft beds and a surprising novelty: a telephone. "You picked it up, heard a foreign language, and put the phone down quickly." Delighted, Thea couldn't help trying it out, again and again.

"All of a sudden we saw things we hadn't seen for a year," Thea recalled. After Zbaszyn, it was hard not to be a bit overwhelmed. "There were these very clean beds, this wonderful food, and this big hall full of people who were saying things in a language you couldn't understand. But they were smiling at you."

However, Thea found some of the food a bit strange. She recalled being served an entire boiled onion with some kind of sauce on it—and not having the words to say she didn't want it.

"I was looking at this and thinking, 'I don't know how to say that I don't want to eat this onion, but I don't want to eat this onion.' Of course, we had no way of expressing what we wanted to say except to push away the plate or to refuse to do what they wanted us to do. So we were upsetting them in many different ways, without meaning to," said Thea. "It was hard, in the beginning, to learn English and to make yourself understood."

FISH AND CHIPS

An only child, Edith Liebenthal had left Vienna, Austria, on a Kindertransport on the Fourth of July in 1939. She always thought of it as her "personal day of independence."

In England, Edith "learned to eat fish and chips, wrapped in newspaper, of course, and Yorkshire pudding; I found out that in every English kitchen there was a pot for drippings; I got to appreciate home-made apple pie (with cloves in it) and deep dish rhubarb pie served with custard."

Edith's family was fortunate: Her parents managed to get visas to work as domestic servants in England,

Jewish refugee children—part of a Kindertransport—from Vienna, Austria, arrive at Harwich, England, December 12, 1938.

where they would stay until their paperwork for the United States was finalized. But it was not a sure thing.

"War clouds were gathering rapidly, and my parents were still in Vienna," Edith recalled. "I knew that they were scheduled to leave on the thirtieth of August, but would they still make it? They did, but it was touch and go. Theirs was the last train to cross from Germany into Belgium."

Edith's parents arrived in England safely, and the family moved to New York in October 1940. Edith immediately found a job and met her husband, Kurt, in 1947. They moved to Houston, Texas, and had three children. Edith and Kurt were married for sixty years before he passed away in 2009.

Edith gave her memoirs to the Leo Baeck Institute in New York in 1995. She wrote, "Every one of us who got out has a story to tell, and those of us who lived to tell it are the lucky ones."

I CRIED FOR THREE DAYS

Harry Heber was in his first year of school when the Nazis appeared in the streets of Innsbruck, Austria. Before long, his father's business had become a target. After the family moved to Vienna, they learned that friends back in Innsbruck had been murdered.

Harry's father heard about the Kindertransport and found places for Harry and Ruth, who were on one of the first trains out of Vienna in December 1938. In England, the siblings were separated. Harry ended up staying with a couple in a remote farmhouse in Sussex that had no electricity or central heating. "Desperately lonely, I cried for three days and nights. The couple couldn't comfort me: they spoke no German, and I had no English."

Like Edith Liebenthal, Harry and Ruth were lucky. "Our parents were also able to find refuge here in the UK, arriving just a few days before the outbreak of World War II," Harry told me in an email. Their rescue was made possible, in part, by his sister's efforts on their behalf. Ruth convinced her host family to sponsor her parents as domestic servants.

The reunion was wonderful, but also bittersweet for Harry's mother. In his months away, young Harry had learned to speak English fluently, but he had lost all his German. "When my mother realized I couldn't understand her, she burst into tears."

Harry and his family settled in England. His father lost his six brothers and sisters in the Holocaust. Harry's grandmother died in Auschwitz. "There was no question of our ever resettling in Innsbruck after the war," Harry said. "We knew good people there, but once you've experienced your friends and neighbors turning against you, how can you ever return?"

Harry now lives in England; he and I spoke on the

phone in 2017. He told me about growing up in Innsbruck and how he felt when the Nazis came. One of his most fascinating stories was how, after his parents had moved to London, they applied some creative ingenuity to make a living. The war was still going on, and everyone was required to have a gas mask to protect against a possible attack. Usually, these were carried around in a cardboard box tied with a string.

"Dad had the idea to use oilcloth," Harry said. So his parents started a cottage industry, working out of their apartment to design and make oilcloth cases for civilians to carry their gas masks. The cases caught on. "They became a fashion item," Harry remembered with a laugh.

After the war, Harry's sister trained as a fashion designer; Harry embarked on a long and successful career as an optician. He has used his skills to help others. Before retiring, he began volunteering for World Jewish Relief, helping to establish a program called the Optical Project to provide glasses to those who can't afford them. By 2007, Harry had provided fifty thousand pairs of glasses to people in fifteen countries.

When I asked his advice for young people today, Harry said, "Be sure to be grateful and love your parents and always look ahead on the bright side.

"The main thing is to be true to yourself."

FIRST RIDE IN A DOUBLE-DECKER BUS

After their long train journey, John Fieldsend and his brother, Arthur, waited uncertainly at Liverpool Street station in London. A woman they soon learned to call Aunty Vera came to collect them. She would be their new foster mother.

When they stepped outside, John got his first shock: one of London's distinctive red buses. A double-decker. "I shall always remember my sense of sheer terror at the double-decker, never having seen one before, which I was completely convinced would turn over!"

John loved anything related to trucks and cars

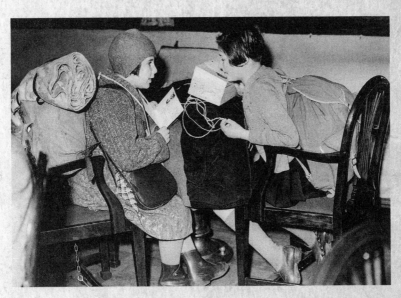

Two Austrian children, part of a group of predominantly Jewish refugee children on a Kindertransport, upon their arrival in Harwich, England, December 12, 1938.

though, and soon was telling everyone that when he grew up he wanted to be a doctor to a motor car. (He didn't: He became a minister.)

LAUGHTER AND TEARS

When Lisa Leist Seiden arrived in England, she was dazed and sleepy from the long journey. She found herself in a large hall at Dovercourt Camp. "We were seated at long wooden tables and in front of each one of us there was a soup plate, a spoon and some bread rolls. I remember that it was very cold so the idea of getting something hot was very comforting, but instead of that, they made us stand up and turn round to face a platform in the center of which there was a microphone and on either side, three empty chairs."

Lisa and her friend Grete were right next to the microphone. The children were welcomed in German, and then a thin, rather curious-looking man began to sing. For some reason, it struck Grete as funny, and she dissolved into a fit of giggles. Giggling can be contagious, and before she knew it, an exhausted Lisa burst into laughter too.

Lisa felt mortified when, at the end of the song, a woman led her and Grete up to the platform. "I put my hands over my face, convinced that we were going to be publicly scolded for our rude behavior."

Instead, the woman addressed the potential foster families who'd come to see the children, saying, "'Look at these poor girls, sobbing their hearts out; how they suffer, touched by the words of our old English song . . .'" And then she appealed for the English people to take in the Kindertransport refugees.

Lisa and her brother, Peter, weren't chosen then. But a few days later a cheerful woman from the city of Bath arrived to take them in. "One moment we were in the [holiday] camp and at the next we were driving off with a strange lady who talked and laughed all the time, oblivious of the fact that we couldn't understand anything she was saying."

That night, in a strange cold house far from home, with the wind knocking branches against the window, Lisa decided she'd had quite enough of this adventure. She wanted to go home.

That, of course, was impossible. Lisa and her family were caught up in something much larger than themselves. "I was yet to learn that my wants and wishes had lost the power they used to have."

A GLOWING ORANGE

Hannele Zürndorfer was thirteen when she left her Vienna home on a Kindertransport on May 3, 1939. The night before, her father wrote poems for the girls' autograph albums. (Hannele's younger sister, Lotte, would grow up to become a poet and literature professor.) Their parents placed their hands on the girls' heads and blessed them as they did each Friday night. It would be the last time.

"It all passed like a dream," Hannele wrote later. She couldn't recall everything, even seeing other parents and children. "I do remember when the unbelievable moment of separation actually came. We were all busy with the preoccupations of finding the right coach and compartment, of stowing the luggage. Then the last clinging embrace: my face against the familiar tweed of my father's coat and the comforting feel of my mother's fur collar."

The girls didn't cry, not until the train pulled out. For Hannele, the journey was mostly a blur. She remembered crossing the North Sea to Harwich, England, by boat; the children then continued on by train to Liverpool Street station in London. There they disembarked to wait for foster families and sponsors and relatives. Lotte and Hannele were luckier than many because they were going to stay at first with an aunt they knew, rather than with strangers.

"The first clear picture that emerges is of our arrival very early in the morning at Liverpool Street Station, a vast glass dome swirling with steam, and of filing through a door into a great hall with windows high up in the walls and a gray light filtering through them. As we entered, our names were checked off a list and we were each given a packet of sandwiches, some chocolate and an orange," said Hannele. She remembered the orange particularly. It cheered her up: "round and brightly glowing in the gray surroundings."

Hannele and Lotte adjusted well. Later, after the war began, the sisters were evacuated from London and sent to the countryside along with thousands of English children. Foster families from the nearby villages came to inspect the children who needed a safe place to stay, away from the threat of bombing raids in London.

Some of the families didn't want to take in German refugees, and it was also hard to place two sisters together. Eventually, someone chose Hannele and Lotte. But the girls were miserable with this family. When their aunt in London sent them a postcard written in German, their new foster father took it away without letting the girls read it. Hannele wondered if he suspected them of being spies.

For a while, they received letters from home. Hannele's father wrote to give her advice about studying hard in school; he reminded her to be grateful and polite. Hannele realized her parents were no closer to being able to leave Germany. Like so many others, they had to wait for paperwork, for affidavits from relatives in America; for their number to come up. Their hopes were crushed again and again.

FRIEDA'S YO-YO

One of the few things Frieda Korobkin had slipped into her suitcase was the yo-yo her grandfather, whom she called Opa Shmuel, had once brought home to her. He was a modest man—so modest he was known for walking with his eyes fixed on the ground. In fact, he claimed to have found many valuable objects this way. Even as a little girl, Frieda had her doubts about this. After all, his finds had included ribbons for her sister's hair and matching colorful yo-yos for her brother and herself.

Frieda was from an Orthodox Jewish family. And while her first foster family in England kept a kosher household, they didn't follow Jewish customs in the same way. Soon after her arrival, for instance, Frieda felt uncomfortable being taken to a movie on a Saturday, something that wouldn't have been permitted in her home on Shabbes, the Jewish Sabbath.

To make matters worse, Frieda couldn't understand much of what was being said in English. Eventually, exhausted, she dozed off in the comfortable seats.

She woke up when her foster mother gave her a sharp blow on the side of her head. She also got a fierce tongue-lashing for wasting the family's money by falling asleep.

Frieda was unhappy, but there was no one she could tell. Once a week, her sister Mimi, who was living with a different family, was brought over for a short visit. Frieda remembered the pain of those meetings. "We are not left alone together for a moment so I cannot tell Mimi how Mrs. Simmons, with a look of disgust on her face and pinching her nose with one hand, made a bundle of all my clothes and threw them into the rubbish together with my tattered suitcase, which still contained the yo-yo Opa Shmuel gave me."

DO YOU WANT A FIGHT?

In June 1939, Alfred Traum and his sister, Ruth, traveled to England on a Kindertransport. Language proved to be a problem, and it got Freddie into trouble right away.

"The following Monday morning, after our arrival in London, I was enrolled in the local school and placed in a class appropriate for my age. I spoke only several words of English, which was just enough to get me into trouble.

"When one of the boys asked me, 'Do you want a

fight?' I used the one English word in my lexicon and answered, 'Yes.'

"I wasn't sure what he wanted of me, but was certainly shocked and surprised when he punched me. I quickly learned that I had to improve my language skills."

Chapter Twelve
NEW LAND, NEW LIVES

Leslie

A COLD HOLIDAY CAMP

Leslie Brent arrived in England in early December 1938, on the first Kindertransport. In the rush to respond to the dire situation in Germany, there hadn't been time to advertise and secure homes for all the children. Instead, the organizers rented a summer camp outside the port of Harwich near the beach. Dovercourt Camp would be the first stop for many of the refugees, and a place to stay until more permanent situations could be found for them.

While Dovercourt might've been delightfully pleasant in summer, the winter of 1938–1939 was cold and snowy. The small wooden chalets had no heat. The

Jewish refugee children from Germany—part of a Kindertransport—at the holiday camp at Dovercourt Bay, near Harwich, shortly after their arrival in Great Britain in 1938.

dining hall was equipped with just an old-fashioned iron stove. All the children who spent time at Dovercourt shared one clear memory: It was cold!

To let the public know about the need for foster families, the BBC (British Broadcasting Company) produced a radio show about the Kindertransport refugees. Years later, Leslie Brent was able to track down a recording of the program and hear his own voice. Since he'd learned a fair amount of English (from that Nazi teacher not exactly pleased with his progress), Leslie had been asked to give a little speech about the daily routine at Dovercourt. This is what he said:

"A bell rings at eight o'clock and we have to get up. Some boys get up earlier to make a run to the sea, which is near the camp. At 8:30 we have a good English breakfast, which we enjoy. First we did not eat porridge but now we like it. When we finish the breakfast we get the letters or cards from our parents, and we are all very happy. After that we clear and tidy our rooms, then we have two hours [of] lessons in English. When the lessons are over we take our lunch and then we can make what we like.

"After tea we can go to the sea, which is wonderful, or we play English games of football. In the evening we learn a lot of English songs till we go to bed. I sleep in a nice little house with two other boys. Now it is very cold and we cannot stay in our house. We like to sit around the stove in a very large hall, and we read or write to our parents.

"The people are very kind to us. . . . Sometimes we go to a picture house in Dovercourt. We have seen the good film *Snow White and the Seven Dwarfs*. We were all delighted. Now I will go to school, then I can speak English good and then I would like to become a cook. We are all very happy to be in England."

LOOK, LISTEN, REMEMBER: You can hear Leslie's voice too. Excerpts from the 1938 BBC recording, including Professor Leslie Brent speaking of his memories of his boyhood, can be heard at: https://www.bbc.co.uk/radio/play/b0075mvb. Leslie as an adult can be heard around the four-minute mark, and at about twenty-six minutes into the program you'll hear his voice as a child in 1938.

Marianne

THE HORRORS OF HOMESICKNESS

Unlike Thea Feliks Eden, Marianne Elsley had something to eat more appetizing than an onion when she first arrived in England. After her long journey, Marianne found herself in the hall of a London train station. It was a cold gray day in February, and she felt a little like a swallow on a wire, crammed in closely beside the other children. They all peered anxiously at the benches on the other side of the hall where foster parents and sponsors had gathered.

"Some of the little children were suddenly overcome with terror at the sight of all these strangers who could not speak their language, and screamed and clung to us older ones," Marianne recalled.

Marianne's foster mother turned out to be a kind woman named Mrs. Carter. The first place they stopped was a famous British restaurant called Lyons Corner House. "This was my first English dinner and I thought every mouthful of it was delicious," said Marianne. "We had wafer thin slices of roast beef, Yorkshire pudding [a traditional side dish], roast potatoes and very dark green boiled cabbage, and I considered it the best meal I had ever had. The dinner really got us off to a good start; Mrs. Carter was a very wise woman." The members of Marianne's foster family were Quakers, a religious group with a long tradition of helping refugees, then and now.

Despite this warm welcome, Marianne felt terribly lonely. "It is impossible to describe the horrors of homesickness to anyone who has not suffered from it, and the pain that gnaws at one's soul is not easily

A Jewish girl, wearing a numbered tag, sits on a staircase with her head in her hand after her arrival in England with the second Kindertransport, December 1938.

forgotten. I tried to grit my teeth and behave sensibly.... But, oh, how I missed my parents, my darling mother especially, how I worried and fretted about them, and cried myself to sleep night after night.

"Just as well, that I did not know how perilous the political situation was at that time, that one crisis followed another.... At nine o'clock precisely each night I was sent off to bed, just before the news broadcast, and they succeeded in keeping me at arm's length from the realities of the impending war," Marianne wrote.

"Right from the start I was determined to like England and to accept whatever I came across ... I really don't know how I managed this, and I certainly was not conscious of doing so. Anything that might have struck me as peculiar I simply put down to being how the English did it, and that was all right as [far as] I was concerned.

"For instance, only an evening or so after my arrival a man came and fitted me for a gas mask. No explanations were given, and I did not ask questions. Naturally I assumed that this was an English custom, and if they liked to own little square boxes containing respirators, that was fine as far as I was concerned. It did not occur to me that this might have anything to do with the country I had just left.

"I did speak to [my parents] on one occasion before the war. My birthday is in June and my parents cautiously proposed that they should try to ring me up on that evening," Marianne recalled. "It is hard to describe how difficult an enterprise this was. My parents did not have a phone at home, so they had to make the call from a post office, or a friend's house. Public call-boxes were watched and tapped in those days, and it was not so easy to make calls abroad then as it is now . . .

"Finally, and after a good deal of explaining and underlining of words, seven p.m. our time was agreed on. It really would not have mattered. I was ready and waiting from about five o'clock on, and when seven came I felt quite sick. However, punctually at seven the call came through, and we spoke to each other for three minutes. It was the last time I heard their voices."

Ruth

WE WAITED WITH LONGING

Ruth arrived in Harwich, England, on June 7, 1939. She had a child's ID and a number: 6295. "I was confused. One of my suitcases was with me, the other larger one had vanished. Suddenly I saw it standing on a platform, looking as forlorn as I felt. I made my lonely way to pick it up, and joined the other children in the train to Liverpool Street Station, London ... Was it my misery that made Liverpool Street look dirtily dreary, gray and unwelcoming?"

Ruth was lucky to be able to spend a few days in London with people who spoke German before going to a more permanent home in a hostel. London was a shock. Her village had only a few cars and no paved roads. The traffic felt overwhelming. In fact, when Ruth read an early draft of this book, she wrote to tell me she also recalled being totally astonished by her first sight of London's famous buses. "A fantastic vision really! I longed for a ride."

Soon Ruth was on another train, this time to Tynemouth, a small seaside town in northeast England. Ruth had never lived by the sea. Now it seemed "huge, infinite and relentless."

Here, people in the local Jewish community had established a hostel for twenty-four girls. Two women, also refugees from the Nazis, served as matrons. One had been the director of a prestigious cooking school in Vienna and managed to create wonderful meals even with the food rationing that was in effect during the war. "If we were lucky, rationing allowed us one egg per week," Ruth recalled. "We never had a whole egg each, but Mrs. Urbach knew how to scramble and add and stretch, so that the weekly egg per person might provide three different suppers for us all."

Originally, the hostel's sponsors thought help would be needed for only six months or a year, just until the girls' parents could manage to get out of Germany. The reality turned out to be far different. Few families were reunited; the war dragged on.

"The Jewish community was not large, and not all its members were in prosperous circumstances. They were to look after us for a long and unexpected seven years, providing a house, food, clothing, care and all the expenses, however modest, that the raising of 24 girls entailed. I owe this community a tribute I have never paid," Ruth reflected years later.

Although they were often sad, the girls adapted, with the older ones looking after the younger ones. At first, they were able to keep in touch with their parents. "In those few months before the war most of us received letters from our families. The mail was the most exciting event of the day, and we all waited for it with longing," Ruth said.

Then on Sunday morning, September 3, 1939, England and Germany went to war, and everything changed.

Chapter Thirteen

LAST TRANSPORT FROM HOLLAND

John Fieldsend and his brother were living with their foster family in the town of Sheffield, England. They were gathered around the radio that Sunday morning. Two days earlier, Germany had invaded Poland. The British had an existing agreement with Poland to protect it if it were ever invaded. For this reason, Great Britain had warned Germany that unless it withdrew its troops from Poland by eleven on September 3, war would follow.

"There was an atmosphere of foreboding in the room," recalled John. "We all fell silent as the radio was switched on. I felt the silence but did not really understand what this was all about."

At eleven fifteen, they heard British Prime Minister Neville Chamberlain announce the news. The deadline for Germany's withdrawal had expired. "'I have to tell you now that no such undertaking has been received and consequently this country is at war with Germany.'"

The outbreak of war meant the end to organized child rescue trains. Sixty children were able to leave Berlin on August 31, just a few days before Great Britain declared war. After that, no more Kindertransport trains left Germany.

Even so, not everyone was willing to give up hope of rescuing more children. Holland had been neutral in World War I, and some people were hopeful that Jewish refugees would be safe there during the war. But German aggression was unrelenting. Germany invaded Denmark and Norway on April 9, 1940. Belgium and Holland were next on Hitler's list.

At three in the morning on May 10, 1940, a middle-aged Dutch refugee worker named Gertrude van Tijn looked up at a dark sky buzzing with German planes. Immediately, she got in her car. The roads were so packed with military vehicles it took her three hours to drive the twenty miles to Amsterdam.

There, she got word that one ship in the northern part of the country, in the port of Ijmuiden, would be available to take Jews to England. All the arrangements had to be made quickly. Another activist, Geertruida van Wijsmuller, who'd been instrumental in getting the original permission from the German Reich for the Kindertransport, set about to locate buses to move Jewish children from a hostel in Amsterdam. It was a desperate situation. There were still thousands of Jews in Amsterdam, many of them refugees from Germany and Austria. This last-ditch rescue effort would save only a few.

But the women did the best they could, getting special travel permits for the buses that would carry the children. Meanwhile, word came over the radio that Queen Wilhelmina of Holland had escaped to England. The nation's government was in exile. There was no military resistance: Holland was simply too small to prevail against the might of Hitler's army.

When Gertrude van Tijn drove to the port, she found a chaotic scene. Many people who wanted to escape couldn't get through. At least, thanks to the permits, the buses with the children were allowed to pass. "About five miles from the quay where the ship was tied up, there were hundreds of cars, bicycles etc. with German and Dutch Jews who were not allowed to proceed to the waterfront. I knew many of them. Some returned to Amsterdam, discouraged. Many just waited and got away later that night, for all night long fishing boats, motor boats, all kinds of small craft left the Dutch coast for England."

After going on board the ship to ensure the children were safe, Gertrude and a coworker disembarked. They stood on the pier, watching as the vessel pulled away. Suddenly some sailors yelled at them to run: The pier was about to be blown up.

"We ran, and almost at once heard a terrific explosion. Looking back, all we saw was a huge cloud of smoke." Luckily, the ship made it through.

"We drove back to Amsterdam; the town was ablaze with lights," wrote Gertrude later. "There was terrible irony in the fact that in this, its darkest hour of her history, Amsterdam was a sea of lights. . . . The next day the Germans reinforced the blackout regulations. The war between Holland and Germany was over. The war against the Jews in Holland was about to begin."

The German Army entered Amsterdam the following morning. "Hour after hour the deserted streets echoed to the tramping of feet and the clanking of tanks. The sky was darkened by planes flying low overhead. I watched from my office window, fascinated and terrified," said Gertrude. "The soldiers seemed to have lost all semblance to human beings. They all looked alike. Young, of perfect physique, they goose-stepped with the precision of robots."

A few of the Jewish children in Amsterdam had been saved. Many more were not, including a young girl about to turn eleven, a girl just two months younger than Ruth David. Her name was Anne Frank.

Earlier, Anne, along with her parents and sister, Margot, had fled Germany for Amsterdam, hoping to be safe from persecution there. In 1942, they went into hiding from the Nazis, along with four others. But a Dutch informer exposed them, and on August 4, 1944, the family was arrested. Anne and her sister were sent to the Bergen-Belsen death camp, where they died. Anne's father, Otto Frank, was the only member of the family to survive.

When Otto Frank returned to Amsterdam after the war, he found Anne's journal. It was published in 1947 as *Anne Frank: The Diary of a Young Girl*. It has been translated into many languages and read by millions. Anne could not have known that her words and her courage in the face of evil would inspire the world.

LOOK, LISTEN, REMEMBER: The Frank family's secret annex hiding place is now a museum. Visit it online at https://www.annefrank.org/en/.

Chapter Fourteen
THE DOOR CLOSES

"'The world war has arrived, and the destruction of Jewry must follow,'" declared Reich minister of propaganda Joseph Goebbels.

The Nazi policy of murdering all Jewish people was called the "Final Solution." On December 12, 1941, just days after the bombing of Pearl Harbor and the entry of the United States into the war, Adolf Hitler gave a speech, announcing a "'clean sweep' to solve the Jewish Question." Jewish men, women, and children would no longer be allowed to leave Nazi-occupied countries through legal means: They would be deported to extermination camps and murdered. Nearly all the parents who sent their children to safety on the Kindertransport suffered this fate.

As the war progressed, a few organizations continued to try to save Jewish children. One was OSE. This Jewish relief organization had been founded by Jewish doctors in Russia in 1912 as the Society for the Health of the Jewish Population. It moved to Paris, France, in 1933, where it became the Children's Aid Organization, or Oeuvre de Secours aux Enfants (OSE). As conditions deterioriated, OSE workers and volunteers focused on saving and protecting Jewish children.

In June 1940, France fell to the Germans and became divided into two parts. The northern part of France was occupied by the Germans. In the south, a regime friendly to Hitler, called the Vichy government, was in charge. OSE moved its activities to the unoccupied southern area of France, though it kept its office in Paris open.

On the surface, OSE ran health care centers and children's homes for orphans. Behind the scenes, however, OSE operated secret escape routes, ran printing labs to produce false-identity papers for people in danger of being arrested, smuggled Jewish children across borders, and arranged for Jewish children to be hidden in non-Jewish homes.

OSE also worked to save children from camps in

Adolf Hitler (lower right) gives the Nazi salute as he reviews victorious German troops in Warsaw, Poland, October 5, 1939, a month into WWII.

France. At first, internment camps for Jews in Vichy (unoccupied) France served as detention centers for refugees fleeing the Nazis. By 1942, however, the Vichy government was allowing the Nazis to deport Jews. In other words, camps that had held refugees became places to hold people before they were sent east to camps like Auschwitz to be murdered. The internment camp system in France became, in the words of historians Dwork and Van Pelt, an "anteroom to Auschwitz."

OSE aid workers desperately tried to find ways to keep children from being deported. They held late-night meetings with officials, trying to find legal loopholes—anything to save lives. At one camp, at the end of August 1942, OSE and other organizations were able to get exemptions for about a hundred children. OSE agreed to take charge of the children and keep them from being sent to an extermination camp. Of course, they also needed the consent of parents.

"'We feverishly notified the parents and obtained, after much persuasion, the authorization to take over the care of the children,'" one aid worker remembered. "'At the moment of separation, the parents proved to be of admirable dignity and calm. Almost all of them informed us of their last wishes, handed their jewels and clothes over to their children, and often expressed their wishes as to their education and future. . . . They asked them to be courageous, worthy of their Jewishness, and not to forget them. And with an abrupt gesture, they turned around to hide their emotion.'"

Not one of these families was ever reunited.

Beginning in June 1941, OSE, the American Friends Service Committee (a Quaker organization), and a group called the United States Committee for the Care of European Children (USCOM), tried to save some children and bring them to the United States. The groups managed to put together five transports, rescuing several hundred children, and were working on paperwork for more.

However, in November 1942, Allied forces invaded Morocco, which was under Vichy control. As a result, the United States broke off diplomatic relations with the Vichy government. All Americans were ordered to leave the area. Another exit route was closed off.

Jewish refugee children, en route to Philadelphia aboard the liner *President Harding*, wave at the Statue of Liberty in June 1939.

OSE also tried to hide individual children. Hiding was difficult both for the family and the child. "A child in hiding could not disclose his identity to anyone," wrote Vivette Samuel, a French social worker with OSE.

"With the loss of his name, which he sometimes tried to forget so as to stay alive, he lost everything that made up his being and his memory. . . . Only one person in the foster family—the mother—knew the true identity of the child she had taken in. To no one else could the child speak [the truth about who he or she was]. He thus lived in perpetual tension. The most sociable child withdrew into himself. A thousand memories haunted him. . . . Rumors reached him about events in which relatives, whose fate he was unaware of, were immersed."

If a child heard talk against Jews, he or she was forced to keep silent—and then was often ashamed of this silence. One of the children Vivette met in her work was a boy named Roger. He was born in Paris in 1928 to Polish parents. Roger was away on a Scouting trip when his parents were warned they were about to be arrested. They tried to escape to the southern unoccupied zone but were caught. Roger ended up being cared for by the secret OSE network; workers found him a place in a foster home and gave him false-identity papers.

Finally, in August 1944, after the Allied invasion of Normandy, Roger could stand the tension no longer. One day he burst out, "'I'm Jewish, and my name is Roger Waksman!'"

∞

Ehud Loeb was a Jewish boy who survived by hiding. Born in Germany in 1934, he was not even seven when he and his parents were put in Gurs internment camp in southwestern France. In February 1941, Ehud's parents entrusted him to the OSE, and he was taken from Gurs into a children's home. His parents were deported to Auschwitz and murdered the following year.

Ehud remained in the children's home for several months. He was "'emaciated, sick, and above all, heartbroken at being separated from my parents. Even today, I remember crying bitterly entire nights.'"

To keep him safe, Ehud was moved, first to a Christian family in a nearby city, and then to a village, under the care of a French couple, Jules and Jeanne Roger. "'He was a butcher; she took care of their fields and garden. Jules Roger was a member of the underground Resistance; his job [as a butcher] entitled him to gasoline, and naturally, his trips by car were made for other purposes,'" Ehud remembered. "'Their house was often full of wounded Resistance fighters, and plans for military operations lay all over the house. At the same time, they were hiding two little Jewish refugees. The other boy, who was younger than I, was a refugee from Poland and Belgium who, like me, had been taken care of by the OSE and placed by them.'"

Jules and Jeanne Roger lived with danger every day. They were fearful of suspicious neighbors who might be informers. "'They faced the risk of being denounced, captured, and shot on the spot,'" Ehud said. "'The

Rogers, who were devout Catholics, never tried to convert me. I was the best student at the catechism, and . . . I played my part of choirboy with great enthusiasm.'"

After the war, Ehud learned that his parents had been killed. OSE helped find a permanent adoptive family for him in Switzerland. Ehud later moved to Israel, where he became an art historian and professor, and a husband and father. In 1989, Jules and Jeanne Roger were recognized as Righteous Among the Nations for the risks they took to hide him from the Nazis.

In reflecting on his own children's lives, Ehud said, "'Strongly conscious of the past, they are free, proud, strong, and confident about the future. They are what I would have liked to have been when I was their age.'"

LOOK, LISTEN, REMEMBER: Righteous Among the Nations is a program to honor those who took risks to save Jews during the Holocaust. It is part of Yad Vashem, the World Holocaust Remembrance Center in Jerusalem. Learn more at the Yad Vashem website: http://db.yadvashem.org/righteous/search .html?language=en.

Voices

LOOKING BACK, MOVING FORWARD

FINDING A JEWISH PATH

The outbreak of war meant more changes for the Kindertransport refugees. Many children in London were sent to new foster families in the countryside for safety during enemy bombing raids on the city, called the Blitz.

For Frieda Korobkin, the change was welcome. Her foster mother hadn't been kind. And one day, with barely a goodbye or an explanation, Mrs. Simmons simply packed a knapsack with Frieda's clothes and brought her to school. From there, the students were bused to the countryside. Once again, Frieda was sent into the unknown on a train, this time to the village of Thorpe. But when the villagers came to select children, Frieda was the last one, left to stand alone on the platform with her teacher after everyone else had been chosen.

Suddenly, a tall, lively lady and a beautiful golden

dog came striding up. Frieda wrote about what happened next. "'I'm Mrs. Whyte-Smith,' she says, 'and this is my dog, Rusty Rufus Reginald Roo, but we call him Rusty, for short. You may pet him, if you like.' Which I do, and Rusty reacts by wagging his tail wildly and slobbering all over my face.

"'Rusty obviously likes you,' says Mrs. Whyte-Smith, 'and any friend of Rusty's is a friend of mine.'"

Frieda loved living with her new foster family, but when they sold their house she had to move again. And then again. A few years later, when Frieda was eleven, she entered Rabbi Solomon Schonfeld's Jewish Secondary School in Shefford. This was a boarding school where most of the teachers as well as the students were refugees.

Frieda was grateful to be one of Rabbi Schonfeld's "Kinder." He had been kind to her since the first day she left home on the Kindertransport. She felt accepted in this thriving Jewish community. Shefford was a turning point, a place where she could recapture a sense of safety and stability.

"Shefford was the place where, for the first time in my life, I did not experience any anti-Semitism. It was the place where my religious observance matured, took root, and flourished, and where the Jewish path that I would follow for the rest of my life, with only a little falter here and there, was laid out for me."

Frieda's memories of the past had begun to fade. "I no longer dreamed of my parents or Oma [her grandmother]. Before going to sleep I tried to conjure up their faces, hoping I would dream of them, but I couldn't remember what they looked like, and I had no photographs."

The end of the war in 1945 brought some hope that Frieda and her siblings might hear news of their family, but that was not to be. They made inquiries through the Red Cross and learned that her parents had reached Yugoslavia, but there the trail ended. At seventeen, Frieda decided to move to Israel and began working. As she walked along the streets, she sometimes found herself scanning faces. She couldn't rid herself of the hopeless fantasy that her parents had somehow escaped.

It was not until 1973, after Frieda had moved to the United States and married, that she finally learned the truth. A mass grave had been uncovered in Yugoslavia; the names of her parents and paternal grandmother were on a list of those killed and buried there. Her parents and others were disinterred and given a proper Jewish burial in Vienna.

Frieda and her husband, Lenny, traveled to Vienna. Frieda was able to visit the apartment building where she'd lived as a young child. And one cold, rainy winter afternoon she went to the cemetery. "It took me some time to locate the grave, and by the time I found it, the rain was coming down in earnest. I had no umbrella and was glad of it. To have been protected from the elements at that moment would, I think, have felt obscene. The stone is a plain flat slab set flush with the earth, which is why it was difficult to find."

Frieda stood in the pouring rain and remembered and prayed.

A DIFFERENT JOURNEY

In England, Frieda found her way to her Jewish roots. John Fieldsend's path took a different turn. In 1947, he decided to be baptized as a Christian, and that same year became a British citizen. He was able to finish schooling and began to pursue a degree in electrical engineering. His brother, Arthur, was completing his medical training. Over time, John realized he was drawn to a religious vocation. He decided to become a minister and was ordained in 1961.

"What I have learnt and constantly had to relearn is that we can't just watch life; inevitably we are on the journey that we call life and on that journey we experience many changes," said John. "We can't choose our starting points and many of the changes are beyond our control."

Living in England changed much for John and his brother. They anglicized their names: from Hans Heinrich (Heini) Feige to John Henry Fieldsend. John's brother, Gert Arthur, became Gerald Arthur Fieldsend. (Fieldsend came about by changing Fei to Fie, then adding something that appealed to them.)

For a while, John and Arthur received letters from their parents. They were able to send photographs of themselves living safely in England, which brought their parents comfort. Later, the brothers learned that their parents, Curt and Trude Feige, had been deported to Auschwitz in February 1943. The dates of their deaths are unknown. Shortly after the end of the war, John and Arthur received a farewell letter from their parents, who, before they were taken away, had given it for safekeeping to a friend.

"'Dear Boys,

"'When you receive this letter the war will be over because our friendly messenger won't be able to send it earlier. We want to say farewell to you who were our dearest possession in the world, and only for a short time were we able to keep you,'" his mother wrote. She then told them of their relatives who had been taken away, knowing that they too would soon be taken.

"'We are going into the unknown; not a word is to be heard from those already taken. Thank the Cumpstys who have kept you from a similar fate. You took of course a piece of your poor parents' hearts with you when we decided to give you away. Give our thanks and gratitude to all who are good to you.'"

Their father added, "'Your dear mother has told you about the hard fate of all our loved ones. We too will not be spared and will go bravely into the unknown with the hope that we shall yet see you again when God wills. Don't forget us and be good.

"'I too thank all the good people who have accepted you so nobly.'"

John Fieldsend married Elizabeth Coles; the couple has three children and seven grand-children. In 2014, John published his memoir, *A Wondering Jew*, and often speaks about the Holocaust in schools and to community groups.

John Fieldsend.

IT TOOK A LONG TIME

For some Kindertransport refugees, letters from parents helped to ease the transition to a new life. But the war made communication nearly impossible, and for most, letters gradually stopped.

Thea Feliks Eden's two older brothers had managed to escape from the internment camp on the Polish border. But Thea lost track of her mother and her younger brother, Leopold, who was called Poldie. "My mother was really on her own. She had that struggle for years until they executed her, essentially. It took a long time to find out how that happened. For some reason I felt compelled to find out where she had died, how she had died, which may not seem terribly rational to people," said Thea.

"What difference theoretically does it make, which concentration camp she died in, or which town she died in, or whatever? But for some reason it made a difference to me. . . . It took about twelve years to find out because the Red Cross didn't know anything after the end of the war."

Eventually, Thea was able to piece together that her mother and Poldie had gotten as far as her mother's original home near the Polish-Russia border. A local doctor told Thea that one day, the Nazis rounded up everyone who was Jewish and shot them. In a way, the news was a relief to Thea. Compared to the horrors of a concentration camp, "Even a bullet became more acceptable, which tells you something about the kind of world we live in."

Thea met her husband, Daniel Eden, in England, and they moved to Israel for a time after the war. Their daughter, Ilana Sharon, was born there. They moved to California in 1963 and worked on restoring houses. Thea's husband died in 1985, and Thea passed away in 1994 after a battle with breast cancer. In her memoir, *A Transported Life: Memories of Kindertransport; The Oral*

History of Thea Feliks Eden, edited by Irene Reti and Valerie Jean Chase, Thea vividly describes growing up under the Nazis in Cologne, Germany, and the horrifying conditions at Zbaszyn.

When asked about the future, Thea was somewhat hopeful that something as horrific as the Holocaust could never happen in the future. At the same time, she warned that it was always possible for hate groups to arise. "Any mass communication brings with it danger, I think," Thea wrote. She urged young people to think for themselves and become well informed about the world.

THE FAREWELL

Family photographs became rare treasures for Kindertransport refugees who later lost their parents. Alfred "Freddie" Traum's father had loved photography. He'd taken some final pictures before Freddie and his sister, Ruth, left Vienna on a Kindertransport.

"When the photograph had been developed, a copy was sent to us in England. It captured all of our feelings. It is the saddest picture I have ever seen; nevertheless, it is a treasured memento of that day. On one of the negatives my father had written *Der Abschied.* The farewell."

Freddie kept two dates close to his heart. The first

was June 20, 1939, the day he and his sister, Ruth, left Vienna for England. The other was June 24, 1958, the day he married.

His sister came from Israel for the celebration and brought a special gift, which she had saved for many years. "It was my father's kiddush cup, the same cup I had seen on so many Friday nights. It came as an utter surprise to me. I had no idea she possessed it.

"Apparently, my father took an enormous risk and stuffed the cup in among my sister's clothing, without telling her but knowing she would know what to do with it and when the moment was right to pass it on to me. That moment had come, my wedding. But more important, my father, in parting with his kiddush cup, which he had most likely received at some special occasion, must have been acutely aware of the severity of his and my mother's situation and the doubtfulness of their survival. It is my most prized possession.

"Every Friday evening, as my family ushers in the Sabbath, the cup graces our table. Perhaps I don't hold it in the same manner as my father did, but I recite the same blessing over the wine and gratefully look around at my family and think how fortunate I am to have had such wonderful parents."

LOOK, LISTEN, REMEMBER: Alfred "Freddie" Traum became an English citizen and served in both the English and Israeli armies. He married another Holocaust survivor and moved to the United States in 1963. He worked for the Boeing Company until his retirement and remains an active volunteer with the United States Holocaust Memorial Museum in Washington, DC.
You can see photos of Freddie then and now by visiting https://www.ushmm.org/online-calendar/event /MAFRSTPERTRAU0618. In 2017, he spoke as part of the USHMM's First Person series: https://www.youtube .com/watch?v=iFOIIE8rT_w.

THEY MIGHT STILL BE OF SOME USE

For Hannele and Lotte Zürndorfer, letters from home also stopped. It would take a long time to piece together what happened. Eventually, Hannele learned that her parents had been deported in October 1941 to the Lodz ghetto in Poland, where her father died on April 26, 1942. For a long time, there was no information about her mother. Today, we know that the girls' mother, Elisabeth, was deported from the Lodz ghetto on May 7, 1942, and arrived in the death camp of Chelmno the following day. She and those with her were gassed on arrival.

A family friend shared news with Hannele about her parents' last days before their arrest. She said Hannele's mother had wanted to commit suicide together rather than be deported to a camp. But Hannele's father had calmed her, saying that they might still be of use to someone. In fact, he used some of his last money to buy a case of medical supplies to take with them.

"'He believed he might be able to help many people there,'" her parents' friend told Hannele.

In 1983, Hannele published a memoir of her early life and escape to England called *The Ninth of November*. She dedicated it to the memory of her parents.

THE BOY IN THE STATUE

Sir Erich Reich was only four when he left Vienna on a Kindertransport and has no real memories of the family he left behind, something which he regrets. He can only wonder what he must have felt upon leaving. "What did I feel in that moment, standing on the precipice of separation from the warmth of parental love and protection? Was I aware, even if only subconsciously, of the new life confronting me in a strange country . . . ?"

Erich was lucky: He grew up in a loving foster family in England. "By making me part of their family, I believe they gave me a sense of belonging, of being loved and wanted, of providing that warm safety net we yearn for during the awkward growing up period, so full of doubts and anxieties. As a consequence, I believe I retained a semblance of emotional stability, which otherwise could so easily have been lost amidst the trauma of the early separation from my parents."

A photograph of Sir Erich Reich inspired the figure of a small boy in the statue of the Kindertransport at Liverpool Street station, made possible by World Jewish Relief and the Association of Jewish Refugees.

Despite the sadness in his early years, Sir Erich Reich persevered, forging a successful career, dedicating time to Kindertransport reunions, and enjoying a rewarding family life. "My instinct has always been to not stay down in the dark for too long, but to get back up as quickly as possible because the scenery is much brighter, more enticing, uplifting and far reaching when seen from above."

IN SEARCH OF A BETTER WORLD

When their first foster family in Bath, England, moved, Lisa Leist Seiden and her older brother, Peter, had a stroke of good luck. In March of 1939 they were taken in by the welcoming and boisterous Hole family, parents with six children who lived on a farm. Their loving care of Lisa and Peter made them feel like a true second family.

"How could we not feel happy at the thought of

living in a full house, full of noise, people, and what is more, to have six playmates around the same age as us?" Lisa wrote later.

Lisa and Peter were fortunate in another way too. Through a family connection, their mother was able to obtain visas for her and their father to go to Buenos Aires in Argentina in the summer of 1939, before the war broke out. However, Lisa and Peter couldn't be reunited with their parents until May 1946, eight years after they left home on the Kindertransport. Lisa had been nine; when she saw her parents again she was seventeen. Once again, she had to leave a familiar place and a foster family she had come to love for another country and a new language.

Lisa was still in England when the war in Europe ended in May 1945. Church bells rang and people ran into the street to celebrate. Lisa reflected, "It was strange that after dreaming about this moment for so long, we were not prepared to live it. . . . It was a glory to know that there were going to be no more blackouts, no more air-raid warnings, no more bombs, no more injured, no more dead, no more tears, no more fears."

That night, the blackout was lifted. Everyone in the city of Bath turned on their lights and threw open the curtains for the first time in years. Lisa and her friends went to the top of a hill overlooking the city. It seemed to her the lights were twinkling like stars, "showing their happiness at the return of peace, the same as the bright rays of the search-lights crossing the skies, now in search of a better world."

Lisa Leist Seiden settled in Buenos Aires, where she worked, married, and raised a family. In 1996, she wrote her memoir, "Thankfully Yours, Lisa Leist Seiden," for her three grandsons and dedicated it to the people of Bath, England, and to her foster family.

From :

✚

WAR ORGANISATION OF THE BRITISH RED CROSS AND ORDER OF ST. JOHN

To :
Comité International
de la Croix Rouge
Genève

Deutsches Rotes Kreuz

21. MAI 1942

ENQUIRER
Fragesteller

Name BUECHLER

Christian name HEINI
Vorname
Address

Relationship of Enquirer to Addressee SON
Wie ist Fragesteller mit Empfänger verwandt ?

The Enquirer desires news of the Addressee and asks that the following message should be transmitted to him.
Der Fragesteller verlangt Auskunft über den Empfänger. Bitte um Weiterbeförderung dieser Meldung.

DEAR PARENTS. HAPPY RETURNS TO
MOTHER'S BIRTHDAY. I AM LEARNING
ENGINEERING VERY GOOD POSITION
LIVING WITH BUECHLER. STEFFI AND
ALFI ARE FINE. LOVE

Date 19.1.42

ADDRESSEE
Empfänger

PASSED

Name BUECHLER

Christian name JACQUES   P.154
Vorname
Address NIEDERWALL STR. 27.
         GLEIWITZ O.S.
         GERMANY.   4 FEV. 1942

The Addressee's reply to be written overleaf. (Not more than 25 words).
Empfänger schreibe Antwort auf Rückseite. (Höchstzahl 25 worte).

A Red Cross letter sent by Heini Buechler to his parents in Gleiwitz.
He had escaped to England on a Kindertransport. His brother,
Alfred, and sister, Steffi, were also saved. Their parents were
murdered during the Holocaust.

244

POSTSCRIPT

The world today is full of wandering people who have fled their homes because they were persecuted, attacked, fearful, starving.

—RUTH DAVID

I did not think I should ever find the courage to read my parents' letters again. For more than thirty years they have been lying in a drawer, securely tucked into an envelope and tied up with a piece of string.

—MARIANNE ELSLEY

I have succeeded in building my life on the foundations laid so lovingly by my parents in my first eleven years. I owe them a huge debt of gratitude, not least in letting go of me when it mattered.

—LESLIE BARUCH BRENT

Marianne
THE SKIES LOOK GRAY

Marianne Josephy Elsley had spoken with her parents once, around her birthday in June 1939, a few months after she arrived in England. She continued to correspond with them over the next few months. Then, in August, just before the war broke out, she received a short letter.

Her father began, "'Beloved child, I want to write a few lines in great haste because the skies look gray and one must expect the worst. I doubt if our emigration papers will come soon enough to overtake events. Mother and I are well. It is a great comfort for us to know that you are in such good hands, and we know that you will always be conscious of the debt you owe to those who have been so good to you.

"'You cannot thank them in any better way than by being, as you have always been, our steadfast and sensible girl and by remaining a good person,'" he went on. "'Perhaps the clouds will pass after all, but it does not look like it. If we should not hear from each other for a time, there will be no cause for alarm on either side.'"

Marianne tried to keep in contact with her parents during the next few years, sometimes through a cousin in Switzerland. The last card in her father's handwriting was dated August 1944. Her parents were sent to Theresienstadt, which was used as a transit camp.

Marianne wrote to her parents there. Her letter was returned. They had been deported in October 1944 to Auschwitz, where they were murdered.

"It is a sad fact that we have come to accept the horror of man's inhumanity to man as commonplace," Marianne wrote.

Marianne trained as a nurse and became a teacher, author, and speaker about the Holocaust. She married Ralph Elsley and had two children. She died in 2009.

Marianne Elsley with her baby daughter, Judy,
in 1952. Courtesy of Judy Elsley.

Leslie

BELOVED BOY!

"Until war was declared I exchanged letters with my parents and sister, but these soon dried up. Alas, only one or two have survived," wrote Leslie Brent.

His parents and sister had applied to the United States consulate for emigration but had a high number: sixty-eight thousand, and, as his father told Leslie, at the time they were dealing with numbers around forty thousand. Things were not working out for his older sister or grandmother to leave either.

Once war was declared, Leslie and his family communicated through special International Red Cross forms, which allowed only twenty-five words for personal messages. Fortunately, Leslie kept many of these, which often began with German words that translated to "Beloved boy!" The messages affirmed that his family was always thinking of him but said little about the trials they were facing in Berlin.

In late October 1942, Leslie received a final message, which contained "the all-important and ominous phrase 'We are going on a journey . . .'"

Leslie Brent's parents and sister were sent to the Riga ghetto in Latvia on October 26, 1942. After three days on trains, they arrived and were taken to the woods and shot.

"I have in my bedroom photographs of my father,

mother and sister, taken as passport photographs round about the time of my departure from Berlin," wrote Leslie. "When I look at them I want to weep for their terrible and cruel fate, and I try to imagine how life must have been for them in wartime Berlin and how they were savagely transported in sealed cattle trucks to their cruel deaths. . . . My heart bleeds when I think of the state to which these wonderful, cultured and sensitive people had been reduced and degraded."

In England, after his stay at Dovercourt Camp, Leslie Brent went not to a family but to a boarding school called Bunce Court, which was under the direction of a renowned educator named Anna Essinger.

At the age of eighteen, in mid-1943, Leslie volunteered for the British Army, attended officers' school, and left the military in 1947 as a captain. "Looking back on this from a great distance, I am—perhaps stupidly—rather proud of having done that," Leslie said in an email in October 2018. He had wanted "to serve my newly adopted country and to help in the liberation of my family. I was not to know until years later that by the time I enlisted they were already dead, but that wouldn't have affected my decision, on the contrary."

Leslie returned to school and went on to earn a PhD, embarking on a remarkable scientific career as an immunologist specializing in immunology and tissue and organ transplants. He was the junior researcher on a Nobel Prize–winning team in his field. A professor emeritus of the University of London, Leslie has also been active in Holocaust education and lecturing about the Kindertransport.

Leslie has returned to Germany, visiting his hometown, speaking at the dedication of memorials, and attending several reunions of former pupils of the Jewish orphanage that served as his last home before leaving on the first Kindertransport. He has also spoken at the dedication of a memorial to the Kindertransports and children left behind.

While there, Leslie learned about small memorial brass plates called Stolpersteines, which are embedded in pavements outside the last known houses of Jews before they were sent to their deaths. In 2007, Leslie arranged to have these memorials placed for his parents and sister, Eva. Leslie also spoke at the eightieth reunion of the Kindertransport in November 2018.

Although an optimistic person, Leslie worries that humankind has not learned all it could from history. He is concerned about the unjust treatment facing refugees and the failure of the world to tackle global warming. He continues to hope that people will evolve "to be more compassionate and more tolerant."

Ruth

IT SEEMED ENDLESS

"The war continued," Ruth David remembered. "It seemed endless." At her hostel, she and the other girls listened constantly to war news on the BBC. "We gradually understood more English, though at times our frustration was intense, when through lack of language we missed some vital information."

Ruth was thirteen when she came upon a photograph in a magazine that showed the execution of Jewish laborers. It was like the small piece of a jigsaw puzzle, as she attempted to find out what was occurring in the war. "I was afraid for my parents and for all those I knew to be in danger."

Ruth's family was in jeopardy. While her two older brothers had been able to emigrate, and she and her sister Hannah made it to England on the Kindertransport, their parents and youngest siblings, Michael and Feo, were still in Mannheim, Germany.

Eventually, Ruth learned they had been deported to a refugee camp in southwest France in October 1940, where they were forced to live in primitive conditions.

"My parents had been expelled from Germany by the Nazis," Ruth said. They were first sent to a camp in Gurs. "From there they were moved to Rivesaltes as Gurs was hopelessly overcrowded. Rivesaltes was dreadful, in a marshy, swampy mosquito-laden area where people still caught malaria and died."

Ruth received occasional letters, but "my parents never mentioned the dreadful conditions in which they lived, nor the hunger and privations they had to endure."

Ruth's brother Michael was rescued by a Norwegian worker for the American Friends Service Committee named Alice Resch, who brought about fifty children to an orphanage nearby. Michael survived the war.

Her little sister, Feo, remained in the camp with her parents. "But eventually, when a new opportunity of rescue arose, they let her go too." In fact, Feo was rescued by OSE and put in semi hiding. She was only seven. Years later, Ruth said, Feo remembered little of this time. But one letter still exists that she wrote to her parents, saying that she was allowed to eat a whole mandarin orange, a luxury at a time when food was scarce.

On August 11, 1942, Ruth's mother sent her last letter to a cousin in London, with a message for her children. "'I am thinking of you all with intense love. Once again we are facing a new turning point in our destiny and we have to move. . . . think of us in love.'" Ruth's mother and father were deported to Auschwitz on August 17, 1942, where they were murdered.

Ruth David became a teacher and the mother of two children, as well as an author and lecturer. Her older

Ruth David continues to educate young people about the Holocaust and speak out on behalf of refugees.

brothers, Werner and Ernst, along with her sister Hannah, eventually settled in the United States. Michael and Feo survived the war and live in France. Ruth remained in England.

Years later, Michael encouraged Ruth to return to visit their childhood home in the Odenwald. Ruth had mixed feelings but eventually did visit. She began accepting invitations to speak in German schools about her family's experience and read from her memoir, *Child of Our Time.*

"I felt I had a useful role to play there, one I had not expected . . . Teachers and students wanted to know," said Ruth. After she speaks, the room is always silent at first. "The students seem quite stunned, but the questions come. . . . Some can't believe it."

Ruth has always encouraged young people—and teachers as well—to ask their parents and grandparents about this time. Once, a teacher burst into tears, thinking of what it would be like to send her own ten-year-old daughter away forever. Keeping alive the past and helping a new generation understand what happened has been, Ruth once said, "the most useful work I have ever done."

In November 2018, she attended the eightieth reunion of the Kindertransport.

"As with other survivors," Ruth wrote, "the pain and grief live with me still, and always will."

I once read that our stories—our heritage—are the only things that remain when we die. We can leave property, money, jewelry, and other worldly goods, but none of those are truly lasting. The only thing that is constant is the thread of how we got to be who we are, and how our short time on Earth is connected to the people who came before and who will come after us.

—WERNER NEUBURGER

Bernd Koschland lighting a candle for Holocaust Memorial Day.

Here are my final thoughts as I reflect on my experiences. I tried to contact my parents via the Red Cross, but by that time they were already dead. Did I, do I, miss them? Of course, especially and strangely in latter years, when I hear other people saying to parents, for instance: "Can we stay with you?" "Will you come over to us?" "Dad, how do I fix this?"

I believe strongly that despite the past, life must carry on, that you must do something useful with your life. Today, speaking about the Holocaust and the Kindertransport is part of the lives of many who survived. I believe that this is so important, that memories of the Holocaust, and the Kindertransport, are passed on to the next generation and not forgotten.

Genocide still happens today, and its effects are felt by many. For those who survived Auschwitz, the Holocaust, and for the Kinder who lost their families, the aftermath of the Holocaust is still with them. The aftermath is still with me. The Holocaust must never be forgotten. It is now a tragic part of humanity's history despite those who deny that the Shoah happened. It did happen, and we must remember it and never forget.

—**BERND KOSCHLAND**

ABOUT THE PEOPLE IN THIS BOOK

SURVIVORS

WERNER ANGRESS was born in Berlin, Germany, in 1920. He emigrated to the United States at age nineteen and served with the 82nd Airborne Division in the Allied invasion of Normandy on June 6, 1944. He went on to become a distinguished professor of history. He died in Berlin in 2010.

HEDI STOEHR BALLANTYNE was born on April 9, 1927, in Vienna, Austria. Her Jewish father, Richard Stoehr, was a well-known composer and teacher who left the country to teach in the United States. She escaped Austria on a Kindertransport and was reunited with her family. She graduated from the University of Vermont and became a high school teacher, wife, and mother. She also volunteered her time to tutor immigrants. Hedi died in 2018.

PROFESSOR LESLIE BARUCH BRENT is a distinguished immunologist and the author of *Sunday's Child? A Memoir*. He was born in Germany in 1925 and escaped in December 1938. He lives in London. In November 2018, he spoke at the eightieth reunion of the Kindertransport.

RUTH OPPENHEIMER DAVID was born in Frankfurt, Germany, on March 17, 1929, and grew up in a small village. She escaped on a Kindertransport in June 1939. A retired teacher, she is the author of two books about her and her family's experiences, *Child of Our Time* and *Life-Lines*. Ruth lives in Leicester, England, where she still speaks about her experience as a refugee.

THEA FELIKS EDEN was born on August 26, 1926, in Cologne, Germany. She escaped the week that World War II broke out. She died in California in 1994. Excerpts from her memoir are courtesy of Herbooks.

MARIANNE JOSEPHY ELSLEY was born in Rostock, Germany, in 1923. An only child, she was fifteen when she left Germany in January 1939. She died in 2009. Quotations from her unpublished memoir, "Without Bitterness," are included here by permission of the Leo Baeck Institute and her daughter, Judith Elsley. She also published a memoir, *A Chance in Six Million*.

EDGAR FEUCHTWANGER was born in Munich, Germany, in 1924. His family escaped to England, where he became a professor of history. Among his books is the memoir *Hitler, My Neighbor: Memories of a Jewish Childhood, 1929–1939*.

JOHN HENRY FIELDSEND was born Hans Heinrich Feige in 1931. He was one of about seven hundred children from Czechoslovakia rescued thanks to the efforts of Nicholas Winton, Trevor Chadwick, and others, both in England and Prague. John became a Christian minister and is the author of *A Wondering Jew*, which has also been translated into Czech and Portuguese. He lives in England.

RUTH SASS GLASER was born in Düsseldorf, Germany, in 1919 and left Germany in 1936 to train as a baby nurse in Geneva, Switzerland. She immigrated to the United States in 1947 and died in 2008.

HARRY HEBER was born in Innsbruck, Austria, in 1931 and escaped on a Kindertransport in December 1938 with his older sister, Ruth. A retired optician, he lives in England.

FRIEDA STOLZBERG KOROBKIN was born in Vienna, Austria, and escaped in 1938 on a Kindertransport. She lives in California and has three children and many grandchildren.

BERND KOSCHLAND was born in Germany in 1931 into an Orthodox Jewish family and escaped on a Kindertransport in March 1939. His sister followed a few months later, but their parents were murdered during the Holocaust. Bernd married in 1957 and has two children. He also has three married grandsons and two great-granddaughters (as of 2017). A retired teacher, he lives in England and serves as the editor of the Kindertransport newsletter of the Association of Jewish Refugees.

EDITH ROSENTHAL LAVENDER was working in Germany during the book burnings of 1933. She and her husband, Paul Lavender, were married in Amsterdam and immigrated to the United States, where they made their lives in Portland, Oregon. They both died in 2005.

EDITH FRIEDLER LIEBENTHAL was born in Vienna, Austria, on February 24, 1924. She escaped to England on a Kindertransport in July 1939, and her parents managed to get visas to join her in England just before the war broke out in September. The family came to the United States in 1940; Edith married and worked in Texas, where she still lives.

WERNER NEUBURGER was born in Battenberg, Germany, in 1926, and escaped on a Kindertransport on July 6, 1939. He came to the United States in 1940, where he was reunited with his mother. His father had died in 1937 after being held in police custody for filing a complaint about Hitler Youth throwing stones. After serving in the United States Army, Werner went to college and worked in the field of mechanical engineering. He and his wife, Henny, live in New Jersey and have three sons and eight grandchildren.

SIR ERICH REICH was born in 1935 and went to England on a Kindertransport when he was four years old. A successful businessman and philanthropist, he is the author of *The Boy in the Statue*.

FRED ROSENBAUM was born in Vienna, Austria, in 1926. He escaped to England in 1938 on a Kindertransport. His family reunited, and he moved to the United States. He became a business and civic leader in Portland, Oregon, where he founded Camp Rosenbaum to give outdoor experiences to children. He died in 2010.

URSULA ROSENFELD was born in 1925 in a small town in Germany. Her father was killed after Kristallnacht. She lives in Manchester, England.

LISA LEIST SEIDEN was born in Vienna, Austria, in 1929. She and her brother were sent to England in December 1938 on a Kindertransport. She lived in Bath. In 1946, after the war, Lisa and Peter were reunited with their parents, who had immigrated to Buenos Aires, Argentina. Lisa married and in 1996 wrote her memoir, "Thankfully Yours, Lisa Leist Seiden," for her grandchildren in Argentina, where she lives.

ALFRED "FREDDIE" TRAUM was born on March 22, 1929, in Vienna, Austria, and escaped with his older sister, Ruth, on a Kindertransport on June 20, 1939. His parents were murdered in the Holocaust. Freddie married another Holocaust survivor, had three children, and relocated to the United States. He has kept in touch with his English foster family and is a dedicated volunteer for the United States Holocaust Memorial Museum.

HANNELE ZÜRNDORFER wrote a memoir entitled *The Ninth of November* about her experiences in Nazi Germany, her escape on a Kindertransport, and her teenage years in England during World War II.

RESCUERS

TREVOR CHADWICK was born in 1907 and was a teacher who worked with Nicholas Winton in Prague, Czechoslovakia, to save nearly seven hundred children, sometimes getting documents forged to enable them to travel. He died in 1979.

RABBI SOLOMON SCHONFELD was born in 1912 and is credited with rescuing thousands of Jewish children and adults. Born in England, he was the son of a rabbi. He died in 1984. In 2013, he was posthumously named a British Hero of the Holocaust for his rescue work.

GERTRUDE VAN TIJN was born in Germany in 1891. She served as a social worker assisting Jewish refugees in Amsterdam in the 1930s and 1940s. She later moved to the United States and died in 1974 in Portland, Oregon.

NICHOLAS WINTON was born in England in 1909. His work rescuing children from Czechoslovakia was recognized in 1988. He died in 2015 at the age of 106.

NORBERT WOLLHEIM was born in Berlin, Germany, in 1913. He helped organize the Kindertransport rescues in 1938–1939. He was deported to Auschwitz with his family, where he was forced into slave labor. He survived the war and went on to initiate the first successful suit against the company I.G. Farben for forced labor. He died in New York in 1998.

HISTORIANS

While I consulted many books in my research, the work of these historians was invaluable. You can find books by these authors in the bibliography.

DEBÓRAH DWORK and **ROBERT JAN VAN PELT** collaborated on *Flight from the Reich: Refugee Jews, 1933–1946*. Dwork is the director of the Strassler Center for Holocaust and Genocide Studies and the Rose Professor of Holocaust History at Clark University. Van Pelt is a university professor at the University of Waterloo.

SIR MARTIN GILBERT (1936–2015) was a British historian and author who wrote about Winston Churchill and Jewish history, including the Holocaust.

SIR IAN KERSHAW is a British historian considered one of the world's authorities on Adolf Hitler. He is the author of *Hitler: A Biography*.

WILLIAM SHIRER (1904–1993) was an American journalist and war correspondent who lived in Berlin and made broadcasts about the war until 1940 as one of famed radio journalist Edward Murrow's team known as "Murrow's Boys." His book *The Rise and Fall of the Third Reich* won the National Book Award in 1961.

TIMELINE

1918

World War I ends. The war pitted Germany and Austria-Hungary against Britain, France, Russia, and the United States.

1919

The Treaty of Versailles ending WWI imposes harsh conditions on Germany, including steep payment of reparations.

1925

Adolf Hitler publishes the first volume of his political autobiography, *Mein Kampf* (My Struggle).

1926

Hitler Youth is established. It began with six thousand members; by 1938 the group claimed more than seven million members.

1933

Hitler is elected chancellor of Germany. Actions against Jews, including a boycott and the burning of Jewish books, follow.

1935

The Nuremberg Laws take citizenship from German Jews and impose other restrictions.

1938

On March 12, Hitler annexes Austria, an event known as the Anschluss.

On November 9–10, Kristallnacht takes place, with violence against synagogues, Jewish-owned businesses, and Jewish homes. Jewish men are beaten, rounded up, and arrested.

Following Kristallnacht, the British Parliament debates expanding refugee intake; the first children arrive in Harwich, England, on a Kindertransport on December 2.

1939

On September 1, Germany invades Poland; Great Britain declares war on Germany on September 3.

1940

On May 14, Holland surrenders to Germany, putting an end to Kindertransport efforts there and jeopardizing Jews. Germany also invades Denmark, Norway, Luxembourg, Belgium, and France.

1941

Germany invades the Soviet Union in June. On December 7, Japan attacks Pearl Harbor. The United States enters World War II. The Nazis begin to adopt the "Final Solution," the state-sponsored murder of Jews and others.

1944

The Allies invade Normandy, France, on D-Day, June 6, 1944, beginning the effort to retake Europe and defeat Germany.

1945

In late January, Soviet troops liberate Auschwitz death camp, where it is estimated more than a million people died.

Hitler commits suicide on April 30.

Germany surrenders on May 7, ending the war in Europe.

After the atomic bomb attacks on Hiroshima and Nagasaki, Japan surrenders, and World War II ends on September 2.

1946

The British government offers citizenship to Kindertransport refugees who lost their parents.

GLOSSARY

Anschluss

The annexation of Austria by Germany on March 12, 1938.

anti-Semitism

Hostility toward, violence against, or persecution of Jews.

Aryan

People who speak one or more of the Indo-European languages. In Nazi Germany the term was wrongly identified as a race of blond, blue-eyed European people who were considered superior to others.

Auschwitz

A network of main concentration and extermination camps, along with satellite camps in Nazi-occupied Poland.

brownshirts

Nickname for the SA, a Nazi paramilitary group.

fascism

Political ideas and movement that includes a rejection of democratic values and elections; rule by a small elite; extreme militarism; and a strong, authoritarian, and controlling government.

führer

German word for leader or guide. It became a synonym for Hitler in Nazi Germany.

Kindertransport

Children's transports that rescued approximately ten thousand from the Nazis in 1938–1940.

Kristallnacht

Nazi campaign of violent attacks against the Jews from November 9–10, 1938.

Nazi Party

Abbreviation of the National Socialist German Workers' Party (Nationalsozialistische Deutsche Arbeiterpartei).

SA

Abbreviation of Sturmabteilung, or assault division, a Nazi paramilitary group also known as storm troopers or brownshirts. Members of the SA were responsible for many atrocities against the Jews.

Shoah

Hebrew word for the Holocaust.

SS

Abbreviation of Schutzstaffel, a Nazi paramilitary organization.

synagogue

Jewish place of worship.

LOOK, LISTEN, REMEMBER: RESOURCES TO EXPLORE

There are many excellent resources to learn about the Holocaust and World War II. Here are just a few. These are a starting point where you can hear survivors' testimonies and learn more about the Kindertransport, as well as Nazi Germany and the events leading to World War II. Websites and their contents sometimes change, so please consult a librarian or teacher if you need help in locating information if any of these links become out of date.

ANTI-SEMITISM

A Britannica Kids article on anti-Semitism.
https://kids.britannica.com/students/article/
anti-Semitism/316414

The Anti-Defamation League (ADL) has many resources for students, parents, and teachers.

Here is a list of recommended books on a variety of social justice issues.

https://www.adl.org/education-and-resources/resources-for-educators-parents-families/childrens-literature

No Place for Hate: Find out more about ADL's program to help schools commit to being nurturing communities where each person can thrive and learn.

https://www.adl.org/who-we-are/our-organization/signature-programs/no-place-for-hate

1933 NAZI BOOK BURNINGS

United States Holocaust Memorial Museum

https://www.ushmm.org/collections/bibliography/1933-book-burnings#h127

When Books Burn: University of Arizona Library Online Exhibit and Curriculum Resources

http://www.library.arizona.edu/images/burnedbooks/indexpage.htm

1933 Book-Burning Historical Film Footage: Watch footage of the bonfire at Opernplatz in Berlin and listen to the speech of Reich minister

of propaganda Dr. Joseph Goebbels at the book burning on May 10, 1933.
https://www.ushmm.org/wlc/en/media_fi.php?ModuleId=10005852&MediaId=158

THE HOLOCAUST AND JEWISH HISTORY

History of the word *Holocaust*
https://www.huffpost.com/entry/the-word-holocaust-history-and-meaning_n_1229043

Anne Frank House
https://www.annefrank.org/en/

Leo Baeck Institute
https://www.lbi.org/

National Holocaust Centre and Museum
https://www.holocaust.org.uk

United States Holocaust Memorial Museum: Introduction to the Holocaust
https://www.ushmm.org/wlc/en/article.php?ModuleId=10005143

United States Holocaust Memorial Museum: A Learning Site for Students

https://encyclopedia.ushmm.org/content/en/project/the-holocaust-a-learning-site-for-students

United States Holocaust Memorial Museum: The Liberation of Auschwitz

https://www.ushmm.org/information/exhibitions/online-exhibitions/special-focus/liberation-of-auschwitz

University of Southern California Shoah Foundation Visual History Archive

https://sfi.usc.edu/vha

World Jewish Relief

https://www.worldjewishrelief.org/about-us/

KINDERTRANSPORT AND OTHER RESCUE EFFORTS

Great Britain and the Kindertransport at the Jewish Virtual Library

https://www.jewishvirtuallibrary.org/the-kindertransport

Kindertransport at the Wiener Library for the Study of the Holocaust and Genocide

https://www.wienerlibrary.co.uk/kindertransport

Kindertransport Association History

http://www.kindertransport.org/history.htm

Kindertransport in the USHMM Holocaust Encyclopedia

https://encyclopedia.ushmm.org/content/en/article/kindertransport-1938-40

The Kindertransport and Refugees: Holocaust Memorial Day Trust

https://www.hmd.org.uk/learn-about-the-holocaust-and-genocides/the-holocaust/kindertransport-refugees/

Righteous Among the Nations

This is a program of Yad Vashem, the World Holocaust Remembrance Center in Jerusalem, to honor those who took risks to save Jews during the Holocaust. http://db.yadvashem.org/righteous/search.html?language=en

Trevor Chadwick

https://www.thejc.com/news/uk-news/call-to-recognise-the-teacher-who-risked-his-life-to-save-children-1.58122

Read more about forgotten heroes of the Kindertransport.

https://www.theguardian.com/world/2015/jul/03/forgotten-heroes-of-the-kindertransports

http://www.thejc.com/news/uk-news/marking-the-life-of-a-forgotten-heroine-1.445765

Marie Schmolka

https://marieschmolka.org/about-marie-schmolka

Sir Nicholas Winton

https://encyclopedia.ushmm.org/content/en/article/nicholas-winton-and-the-rescue-of-children-from-czechoslovakia-1938-1939

Children Saved from the Nazis: The Story of Sir Nicholas Winton (film)
https://www.youtube.com/watch?v=nT0yPjj0UqQ

BBC Newsnight, Kindertransport: A Journey to Life (film)
https://www.youtube.com/watch?v=XqP0uVSj3bQ

Gertrude Wijsmuller-Meyer
https://www.encyclopedia.com/women/encyclopedias
-almanacs-transcripts-and-maps/wijsmuller-meijer-truus-c
-1896-1978

KRISTALLNACHT

Leo Baeck Institute, Holocaust Survivors Remember Kristallnacht 80 Years Later (film)
https://www.youtube.com/watch?v=14NPBMgQBK8

USC Shoah Foundation: Remembering Kristallnacht
https://sfi.usc.edu/exhibits/remembering-kristallnacht

Yad Vashem: Kristallnacht Exhibition
https://www.yadvashem.org/yv/en/exhibitions
/kristallnacht/index.asp

ORAL HISTORIES AND ARTICLES

PROFESSOR LESLIE BARUCH BRENT
Listen to a BBC radio broadcast about the Kindertransport: https://www.bbc.co.uk/radio/play/b0075mvb. Leslie can be heard around the four-minute mark, and at about twenty-six minutes into the program you'll hear his voice reciting the words from 1938.

RUTH OPPENHEIMER DAVID
Ruth was interviewed by the BBC on September 18, 2012. Watch *Leicester Woman Honoured by Germany for Holocaust Work*. https://www.bbc.com/news/av/uk-england -leicestershire-19641062/leicester-woman-honoured-by -germany-for-holocaust-work

EDGAR FEUCHTWANGER
Edgar speaks about growing up across the street from Adolf Hitler: https://www.youtube.com /watch?v=9GX2OgRzNQ8. Read more about Edgar's life: https://www.bbc.co.uk/news/magazine-20210025.

LION FEUCHTWANGER
Professor Harold von Hofe describes Lion and Marta Feuchtwanger's daring escape: https://libguides.usc.edu/c .php?g=234957&p=1559413.

HARRY HEBER

Watch Harry Heber and his sister, Ruth, talk about the Kindertransport: https://www.worldjewishrelief.org/about -us/kindertransport/726-harry-heber-and-ruth-jacobs.

EDITH LAVENDER

Interviews with Edith and Paul Lavender are available at the Oregon Jewish Museum and Center for Holocaust Education. Read Edith's account of receiving books here: http://www.ojmche.org/oral-history-interviews/edith-lavender-1993?A=SearchResult&SearchID=5120418&Object ID=5304275&ObjectType=35.

PAUL LAVENDER

Here is Paul's oral history interview: http://www.ojmche .org/oral-history-interviews/paul-lavender-1994?A=Search Result&SearchID=5120406&ObjectID=5088949&Object Type=35.

NORBERT WOLLHEIM

Visit USHMM online to watch and listen to Norbert describe his experience of forced labor: https://encyclopedia .ushmm.org/content/en/oral-history/norbert-wollheim -describes-forced-labor-at-the-buna-works-1.

BIBLIOGRAPHY

* Titles of special interest to young readers.

BOOKS

Angress, Werner T. *Between Fear & Hope: Jewish Youth in the Third Reich*. Translated by Werner T. Angress and Christine Granger. New York: Columbia University Press, 1988.

———. *Witness to the Storm: A Jewish Journey from Nazi Berlin to the 82nd Airborne, 1920–1945*. Translated by Werner T. Angress with Christine Granger. Durham, NC: CreateSpace, 2012.

Baker, Leonard. *Days of Sorrow and Pain: Leo Baeck and the Berlin Jews*. New York: Oxford University Press, 1980. First published by Macmillan, 1978.

Bard, Mitchell G. *48 Hours of Kristallnacht: Night of Destruction/Dawn of the Holocaust*. Guilford, CT: Lyons Press, 2008.

Barnett, Ruth. *Person of No Nationality: A Story of Childhood Separation, Loss and Recovery.* London: David Paul, 2010.

*Bartoletti, Susan Campbell. *Hitler Youth: Growing Up in Hitler's Shadow.* New York: Scholastic, 2005.

Baumel-Schwartz, Judith Tydor. *Never Look Back: The Jewish Refugee Children in Great Britain, 1938–1945.* West Lafayette, IN: Purdue University Press, 2012.

Bentwich, Norman. *They Found Refuge: An Account of British Jewry's Work for Victims of Nazi Oppression.* London: Cresset Press, 1956.

Blend, Martha. *A Child Alone.* Portland, OR: Vallentine Mitchell, 1995.

Brent, Leslie Baruch. *Sunday's Child? A Memoir.* New Romney, UK: Bank House Books, 2009.

*Byers, Ann. *Saving Children from the Holocaust: The Kindertransport.* Berkeley Heights, NJ: Enslow, 2012.

The Child Survivors' Association of Great Britain. *We Remember: Child Survivors of the Holocaust Speak.* Leicester, UK: Matador, 2011.

David, Ruth. *Child of Our Time: A Young Girl's Flight from the Holocaust.* London: I. B. Taurus, 2002.

———. *Life-Lines.* London: self-published, 2011.

*Deem, James M. *Kristallnacht: The Nazi Terror That Began the Holocaust.* Berkeley Heights, NJ: Enslow, 2012.

Drucker, Olga Levy. *Kindertransport.* New York: Henry Holt, 1992.

Dwork, Debórah, and Robert Jan Van Pelt. *Flight from the Reich: Refugee Jews, 1933–1946.* New York: W. W. Norton, 2009.

Eden, Thea Feliks. *A Transported Life: Memories of Kindertransport; The Oral History of Thea Feliks Eden.* Edited by Irene Reti and Valerie Jean Chase. Santa Cruz, CA: HerBooks, 1995.

Elsley, Marianne. *A Chance in Six Million.* Banbury, UK: Kemble, 1989.

Engelmann, Bernt. *Hitler's Germany: Everyday Life in the Third Reich*. Translated by Krishna Winston. New York: Schocken Books, 1986.

Evans, Richard J. *The Coming of the Third Reich*. New York: Penguin, 2004.

Fast, Vera K. *Children's Exodus: A History of the Kindertransport*. London: I. B. Tauris, 2011.

*Feuchtwanger, Edgar with Bertil Scali. *Hitler, My Neighbor: Memories of a Jewish Childhood, 1929–1939*. Translated by Adriana Hunter. New York: Other Press, 2017.

Fieldsend, John. *A Wondering Jew*. Oxford, UK: Radec Press, 2014.

*Fox, Anne L., and Eva Abraham-Podietz. *Ten Thousand Children: True Stories Told by Children Who Escaped the Holocaust on the Kindertransport*. West Orange, NJ: Behrman House, 1999.

Friedman, Edie, and Reva Klein. *Reluctant Refuge: The Story of Asylum in Britain*. London: British Library, 2008.

Gerhardt, Uta, and Thomas Karlauf, eds. *The Night of Broken Glass: Eyewitness Accounts of Kristallnacht*. Translated by Robert Simmons and Nick Somers. Cambridge, UK; Malden, MA: Polity Press, 2012.

Gershon, Karen, ed. *We Came as Children*. London: Papermac, 1989.

Gilbert, Martin, *Kristallnacht: Prelude to Destruction*. New York: HarperCollins, 2006.

Gissing, Vera. *Pearls of Childhood*. London: Robson Books, 1994.

*Gold, Michele M. *Memories That Won't Go Away: A Tribute to the Children of the Kindertransport*. Israel: KIP, 2014.

Gottlieb, Amy Zahl. *Men of Vision: Anglo-Jewry's Aid to Victims of the Nazi Regime 1933–1945*. London: Weidenfeld & Nicolson, 1998.

Haffner, Sebastian. *Defying Hitler: A Memoir*. Translated by Oliver Pretzel. New York: Picador, 2002.

Harris, Mark Jonathan, and Deborah Oppenheimer, eds. *Into the Arms of Strangers: Stories of the Kindertransport*. New York: MJF Books in arrangement with Bloomsbury, 2000.

*Hendrix, John. *The Faithful Spy: Dietrich Bonhoeffer and the Plot to Kill Hitler*. New York: Amulet, 2018.

*Hodge, Deborah. *Rescuing the Children: The Story of the Kindertransport*. Toronto: Tundra Books, 2012.

Jason, Philip K., and Iris Posner, eds. *Don't Wave Goodbye: The Children's Flight from Nazi Persecution to American Freedom*. Westport, CT: Praeger, 2004.

Kaplan, Marion A. *Between Dignity and Despair: Jewish Life in Nazi Germany*. New York: Oxford University Press, 1998.

Kershaw, Ian. *Hitler: A Biography*. New York: W. W. Norton, 2008.

Korobkin, Freida Stolzberg. *Throw Your Feet over Your Shoulders: Beyond the Kindertransport*. New York: Devora, 2008.

Laqueur, Walter. *Generation Exodus: The Fate of Young Jewish Refugees from Nazi Germany.* New York: I. B. Tauris, 2004.

Leverton, Bertha, and Shmuel Lowensohn, eds. *I Came Alone: The Stories of the Kindertransports.* Sussex, UK: Book Guild, 1990.

Lixl-Purcell, Andreas, ed. *Women of Exile: German-Jewish Autobiographies since 1933.* New York: Greenwood, 1988.

Milton, Edith. *The Tiger in the Attic: Memories of the Kindertransport and Growing Up English.* Chicago: University of Chicago Press, 2005.

Neuburger, Werner. *Dark Clouds Don't Stay Forever: Memoirs of a Jewish German Boy in the 1930s and 1940s.* Baltimore: PublishAmerica, 2005.

Ney, Peter. *Getting Here: From a Seat on a Train to a Seat on the Bench.* New York: iUniverse, 2009.

Papanek, Ernst, with Edward Linn. *Out of the Fire.* New York: William Morrow, 1975.

Presser, Jacob. *Ashes in the Wind: The Destruction of Dutch Jewry*. Translated by Arnold Pomerans. London: Souvenir, 2010.

Reich, Sir Erich. *The Boy in the Statue: From Wartime Vienna to Buckingham Palace*. Manchester, UK: i2i, 2017.

Samuel, Vivette. *Rescuing the Children: A Holocaust Memoir*. Translated and with an introduction by Charles B. Paul. Foreword by Elie Wiesel. Madison: University of Wisconsin Press, 2002.

Saville, Annette. *Only a Kindertransportee*. London: New Millennium, 2002.

Semelin, Jacques, Claire Andrieu, and Sarah Gensburger, eds. *Resisting Genocide: The Multiple Forms of Rescue*. Translated by Emma Bentley and Cynthia Schoch. New York: Oxford University Press, 2013.

Shirer, William L. *The Rise and Fall of the Third Reich*. New York: Fawcett Crest, 1960.

Turner, Barry. . . . *And the Policeman Smiled: 10,000 Children Escape from Nazi Europe*. London: Bloomsbury, 1990.

*——. *One Small Suitcase*. New York: Puffin, 2003.

Wicks, Ben. *No Time to Wave Goodbye*. Toronto: Stoddart, 1988.

Wolman, Ruth E. *Crossing Over: An Oral History of Refugees from Hitler's Reich*. New York: Twayne, 1996.

Zeller, Frederic. *When Time Ran Out: Coming of Age in the Third Reich*. Sag Harbor, NY: Permanent Press, 1989.

Zürndorfer, Hannele. *The Ninth of November*. London: Quartet Books, 1983.

ORAL HISTORY INTERVIEWS AND UNPUBLISHED ACCOUNTS AND MEMOIRS

Ballantyne, Hedi Stoehr. "The Last Carefree Summer." Courtesy of the Leo Baeck Institute, New York, 1998.

——. "Draft 5, October 10, 1998." Courtesy of the Leo Baeck Institute, New York, 1998.

David, Ruth. "Another Kindertransport Memorial." Courtesy of the author, ND.

——. "Leaving Germany." Courtesy of the author, ND.

——. "Readings in German Schools." Speech, April 12, 2002.

Elsley, Marianne. "Without Bitterness." Courtesy of the Leo Baeck Institute, New York, ND.

Fontheim, Ernest G. "A Personal Memoir of Kristallnacht." Courtesy of the Leo Baeck Institute, New York, 1998.

Glaser, Ruth Sass. "Düsseldorf Revisited." Courtesy of the Leo Baeck Institute, New York, 1984.

Koschland, Bernd. "Bernd Koschland," Holocaust Memorial Day Trust, https://www.hmd.org.uk /resource/bernd-koschland/.

Lavender, Edith Rosenthal. Edith Rosenthal Lavender (1913–2005) oral history interview by Eric Harper.

Transcribed by Judy Selander. November 3, 1993. Oregon Jewish Museum and Center for Holocaust Education.

Lavender, Paul. Paul Walter Lavender (1911–2005) oral history interview by Eric Harper. Transcribed by Judy Selander. June 24, 1993. Oregon Jewish Museum and Center for Holocaust Education.

Liebenthal, Edith. "Everyone Has a Story to Tell—This Is Mine." Courtesy of the Leo Baeck Institute, New York, 1995.

Rosenbaum, Fred M. "One Child's Lonely Passage to Freedom 1938–1939." Courtesy of the Leo Baeck Institute, New York, 2003.

Seiden, Lisa Leist. "Thankfully Yours, Lisa Leist Seiden." Courtesy of the Leo Baeck Institute, New York, 1996.

Traum, Alfred. "The Gas Mask." United States Holocaust Memorial Museum, 2013.

——. "The Kiddush Cup." United States Holocaust Memorial Museum, 2011.

———. "Vienna, Chanukah, 1938." United States Holocaust Memorial Museum, 2016.

van Tijn, Gertrude (Judy). "Oh Life of Joy and Sorrow." Courtesy of the Leo Baeck Institute, New York, 1959.

Winton, Nicholas, interview by Shoah Foundation Institute for Visual History and Education, University of Southern California, July 6, 2015.

Wollheim, Norbert. Interview with Norbert Wollheim, May 10, 1991. RG-50.030*0257. United States Holocaust Memorial Museum.

———. Interview with Norbert Wollheim, February 18, 1992. RG-50.042*0032. United States Holocaust Memorial Museum.

NEWSPAPERS, ARTICLES, AND WEBSITES

BBC. "1939: Britain and France Declare War on Germany." On This Day: September 3, http://news .bbc.co.uk/onthisday/hi/dates/stories/september/3 /newsid_3493000/3493279.stm.

BBC. "Leicester Woman Honoured by Germany for Holocaust Work." September 18, 2012, https:// www.bbc.com/news/av/uk-england-leicestershire -19641062/leicester-woman-honoured-by-germany -for-holocaust-work.

British Library. "Anti-Jewish Decrees." http://www .bl.uk/learning/histcitizen/voices/info/decrees /decrees.html.

British Parliament. "Racial, Religious and Political Minorities." Speeches in Parliament, November 21, 1938, https://api.parliament.uk/historic-hansard /commons/1938/nov/21/racial-religious-and -political-minorities#S5CV0341P0_19381121 _HOC_436.

Children of Chabannes. https://childrenofchabannes
.org/about-the-ose.

Diez, Georg. "How the Nazis Ruined Erich Kästner's
Career." *Spiegel Online*, April 18, 2013, http://www
.spiegel.de/international/zeitgeist/nazi-book
-burning-anniversary-erich-kaestner-and-the
-nazis-a-894845.html.

Green, Emma. "A Broken Jewish Community." *The
Atlantic*, October 28, 2018, https://www.theatlantic
.com/politics/archive/2018/10/broken-jewish
-community/574216/.

Heber, Harry. "Kindertransport Saved Me from the
Nazis." *The Guardian*, November 3, 2007, https://
www.theguardian.com/theguardian/2007/nov/03
/weekend7.weekend3.

Hsuan, Amy. "Fred Rosenbaum, Oregon Leader,
Philanthropist and Holocaust Survivor, Dies."
The Oregonian, January 12, 2010, https://www
.oregonlive.com/portland/index.ssf/2010/01
/post_11.html.

Keller, Helen in "Helen Keller Warns Germany's Students; Says Burning of Books Cannot Kill Ideas." *New York Times,* May 10, 1933, https://timesmachine.nytimes.com/timesmachine/1933/05/10/105133329.html?action=click&contentCollection=Archives&module=ArticleEndCTA&region=ArchiveBody&pgtype=article&pageNumber=10.

SOURCE NOTES

Note: Excerpts from oral histories and unpublished manuscripts are courtesy of the following organizations: the Leo Baeck Institute, New York (LBI); the Center for Jewish History (CJH); the United States Holocaust Memorial Museum (USHMM); the Visual History Archive of the USC Shoah Foundation, the Institute for Visual History and Education; and the Oregon Jewish Museum and Center for Holocaust Education (OJMCHE). The first citation follows the format requested by the source; in subsequent citations, sources are abbreviated.

PROLOGUE
"Tears kept welling up . . .": Elsley, *A Chance in Six Million*, 39–40.

EPIGRAPHS
"I know very well . . .": Glaser, "Düsseldorf Revisited," courtesy of the Leo Baeck Institute, New York, 1.
"'Think of us.'": Elsley, *A Chance in Six Million*, 118.

INTRODUCTION
"All those present joined in . . .": Traum, "Vienna, Chanukah, 1938," United States Holocaust Memorial Museum.

Part One

"Dort wo man . . .": Heine, H. *Almansor*. Accessed through the Gutenberg Project, http://www.gutenberg.org/ebooks/45600. Originally published in 1821. Gutenberg edition May 7, 2014.

"Crisis was Hitler's oxygen . . .": Kershaw, *Hitler*, 125.

"When the Nazis proclaimed . . .": Bentwich, *They Found Refuge*, 9.

CHAPTER ONE

"to serve my newly adopted country . . .": Brent, email to author, October 24, 2018.

seven-year term: Kershaw, 226.

"Carrying in each hand . . .": Brent, *Sunday's Child?*, 8.

"He had been a soldier . . .": ibid., 9.

"To this day I have . . .": ibid., 11.

"We made our own . . .": ibid., 12.

"It was indeed . . .": ibid., 13.

"These were eaten cold . . .": Elsley, "Without Bitterness," LBI, 12.

"a crunchy, creamy . . .": ibid.

"I remember being allowed . . .": ibid.

"My father, her youngest son, always . . .": ibid., 11.

"The Odenwald forests . . .": David, *Child of Our Time*, 3.

"I knew that my family . . .": ibid.

"She always joyfully . . .": ibid., 14.

VOICES: LIFE BEFORE THE NAZIS

"I shall start . . .": David, "Readings in German Schools," 2.

"Oh, those memories . . .": Seiden, "Thankfully Yours, Lisa Leist Seiden," LBI, New York, 4.

"Sometimes when passing . . .": ibid., 6.

"Sometimes he allowed . . .": ibid.

"I could discover castles . . .": ibid., 7.

"When I called my . . .": ibid.

"Preparing for the Sabbath . . .": Traum, "The Kiddush Cup," USHMM.

"Although he never trained . . .": ibid.

"One day when I was sitting . . .": Ballantyne, "The Last Carefree Summer," LBI, 3.

"We had no bathroom . . .": ibid., 2.

"I would accompany her . . .": ibid., 1.

CHAPTER TWO

"He shouted and raved . . .": Ballantyne, "Draft 5, October 10, 1998," LBI, 4.

"It can be said with certainty . . .": Kershaw, xxviii.

"Behind all evil . . .": ibid., 91.

"His audiences loved it . . .": ibid., 92.

Mein Kampf publication and background: ibid., 147.

"Almost 6½ million Germans . . .": ibid., 204.

March election: ibid., 277.

"the dangerous leader . . .": ibid., 256.

"The whole tradition . . .": Haffner, *Defying Hitler*, 230.

New restrictions: Kershaw, 291.

"'The end of German Jewry . . .'": Baker, *Days of Sorrow and Pain*, 145.

"'Hitler's a thug . . .'": Feuchtwanger, *Hitler, My Neighbor*, 15.

"Waves of Nazis . . .": ibid., 60–61.

"He's right in front of us . . .": ibid., 43–44.

"'But where would we go?'": ibid., 78.

CHAPTER THREE

"Gradually more and more . . .": David, *Child of Our Time*, 14.

"My grandmother had belonged . . .": ibid., 13–14.

"Those monstrous, threatening flags . . .": ibid., 15.

"I was afraid of dogs . . .": David, email to author, October 23, 2018.

"On this day, German mothers . . .": Elsley, "Without Bitterness," LBI, 16.

"One walked in constant fear . . .": ibid., 2.

"The security of my own . . .": ibid., 22.

"They were simply not allowed . . .": ibid.

"I remember one occasion . . .": ibid., 24.

"innocent, calm, comfortable days . . ."; "a worryingtime . . .": ibid., 20.

"Non-Jewish Germans who had been friends . . .": Brent, 18.

"Eva and I watched . . .": ibid., 19.

"'And when Jewish blood . . .'": ibid.

CHAPTER FOUR

"We started French . . .": Lavender, E., transcript, Edith Lavender (1913–2005) oral history interview by Eric Harper. Transcribed by Judy Selander. November 3, 1993, OJCMHEC, 5.

"There was nobody to come in . . .": ibid., 17.

"'Can't you replace . . .'": ibid., 6.

"'Yes, as soon as you get me . . .'": ibid.

"I was sitting in a place . . .": ibid.

"He called me and said . . .": ibid., 7.

"So I went that night . . .": ibid.

Warburg Library: Dwork and Van Pelt, *Flight from the Reich*, 20–21.

"'There's Kästner!'" Diez, "How the Nazis Ruined Erich Kastner's Career."

"'The soul of the German people . . .'": Shirer, *The Rise and Fall of the Third Reich*, 333.

"'History has taught you nothing . . .'": Keller, "Helen Keller Warns Germany's Students . . .".

"Uncle Lion won't ever return . . .": Feuchtwanger, 93.

"Readers . . . were deprived . . ."; "felt intimidated and pushed . . .": Haffner, 196.

"Many journals and newspapers . . .": ibid.

German academics: Shirer, 347.

"'The German universities failed . . .'": ibid.

"The temptation to do this . . .": Haffner, 198.

"'South Africa? You're coming . . .'": Lavender, E., OJCME, 9.

"When I introduced myself . . .": ibid., 7.

"Hate is something . . .": Lavender, P. Paul W. Lavender (1911–2005) oral history interview by Eric Harper. Transcribed by Judy Selander. June 24, 1993, OJCMHEC, 19.

"'You are half Jewish . . .'": Ballantyne, "Draft 5, October 10, 1998," 3–4.

CHAPTER FIVE

"My teacher wore a brown uniform . . .": David, *Child of Our Time*, 16.

"I understood enough . . .": ibid.

"Without a word . . .": ibid., 21.

"There is still a vivid picture . . .": ibid.

"What concerned people above all . . .": Kershaw, 341.

"LITTLE BY LITTLE . . .": Baker, 200.

J stamp: Dwork and Van Pelt, 160–61.

"'I don't straight away . . .'": Kershaw, 348.

"When the order came out . . .": David, *Child of Our Time*, 38.

"swore at them loud . . .": David, email to author, October 23, 2018.

"I could not come to terms . . .": David, *Child of Our Time*, 38.

"So Mina, who never lost touch . . .": ibid., 39.

"He was thoroughly steeped . . .": Elsley, "Without Bitterness," 6.

"We were thunderstruck . . .": ibid., 24.

"The time had come . . .": ibid., 25.

"It was he, ironically . . .": Brent, 20.

"My father was reduced . . .": ibid., 27.

"The orphanage was stormed . . .": ibid., 25.

"There we stayed . . .": ibid.

VOICES: THE SIGNS WERE ALL THERE

"Later in the United States . . .": Angress, *Witness to the Storm*, 79–80.

"If I had been older . . .": ibid., 82.

"Naïve as we (and many adults) . . .": ibid., 99.

"At least during the beginning . . .": ibid.

"In a low voice . . .": ibid., 128–29.

"My brother and I . . .": Fieldsend, *A Wondering Jew*, 17–18.

"'That needs stitching . . .'": ibid. 19.

"So late one night . . .": ibid.

"And at the blink . . .": ibid., 26.

"Every few months . . .": Glaser, LBI, 14.

"While I was in school . . .": ibid., 18.

"The Austrians were even more . . .": David, email to author, October 23, 2018.

"My father sold bed linen . . .": Heber, Harry, "Kindertransport Saved Me from the Nazis," *The Guardian*, November 3, 2007.

"Soldiers paraded through the town . . .": ibid.

"You couldn't go out . . .": Heber, phone conversation with the author, November 7, 2017.

"Vienna was quite literally . . .": Liebenthal, "Everyone Has a Story to Tell—This Is Mine," Courtesy of the Leo Baeck Institute, New York, 6.

"The requirement was . . .": ibid., 7–8.

"the situation was getting worse . . .": ibid., 8.

"It went on and on . . .": Traum, "The Gas Mask," USHMM, 1.

"'Go home . . .'": Seiden, LBI, 2.

"'It's because we are Jews.'": ibid.

"Nothing in my appearance . . .": ibid.

Overcrowding law: Gottlieb, *Men of Vision*, 98.

1938 law: British Library, "Anti-Jewish Decrees": http://www.bl.uk /learning/histcitizen/voices/info/decrees/decrees.html.

"As I kneeled . . .": Ballantyne, "The Last Carefree Summer," LBI, 4.

"As I walked home . . .": Ballantyne, "Draft 5, October 10, 1998," LBI, 4.

Part Two

"I don't think evil . . .": Eden, *A Transported Life*, 25.

THE TIPPING POINT 1938

"'It is late at night . . .'": Nathorff, Hertha in Gerhardt and Karlauf, *The Night of Broken Glass*, 148.

Deportation of Polish-born Jews: Gilbert, *Kristallnacht*, 23.

Number killed during Kristallnacht: ibid., 13.

CHAPTER SIX

"I was aware only of a magic glow . . .": Zürndorfer, *The Ninth of November*, 29.

"their light seemed to grow . . .": ibid., 31.

"There was the best china . . .": ibid., 34.

"My favorite shop . . .": ibid., 39.

"At first I only sensed . . .": ibid., 46.

"I wanted to shut out . . .": ibid., 58–59.

"It must have been three . . .": ibid., 70.

"Seconds later there burst . . .": ibid., 60–61.

"Now fear became a living thing . . .": ibid., 61.

"'Children don't look . . .'": ibid., 62.

VOICES: KRISTALLNACHT

"This went on and on . . .": Seiden, LBI, 11.

"'I cannot write them down . . .'": ibid.

"The encounters with my father . . .": ibid., 12.

"The Vienna of my childhood . . .": Korobkin, *Throw Your Feet over Your Shoulders*, 1.

"First they break the windows . . .": ibid., 18.

"I went to my synagogue . . .": Wollheim interview, USHMM, May 10, 1991, 12.

"I couldn't comprehend it . . .": ibid., 13.

"After about a half hour . . .": Rosenbaum, "One Child's Lonely Passage to Freedom," LBI, 3.

"Luckily, I was standing . . .": ibid.

"Thousands of Jews . . .": ibid., 4.

"When I entered my classroom . . .": Fontheim, "A Personal Memoir of Kristallnacht," LBI, 2.

"Firefighters were hosing down . . .": ibid., 3.

"In my imagination . . .": ibid., 4.

"I left this scene of horror . . .": ibid.

"'They had thrown all . . .'": Bard, *48 Hours of Kristallnacht*, 141–42.

"'My father was quite . . .'": ibid., 91.

CHAPTER SEVEN

"I woke to thunderous . . .": David, *Child of Our Time*, 41–42.

"The unexpected happened . . .": ibid., 42.

"I cannot say today how long . . .": ibid.

"Today I am still trying . . .": ibid., 43.

"Now each jar lay . . .": ibid.

"It was clear that . . .": ibid., 46.

Ruth's father's arrest: David, email to author, October 23, 2018.

"The ring at the door . . .": Elsley, "Without Bitterness," 3.

"They did not believe me . . .": ibid.

"I stood there in terror . . .": ibid.

"In those days . . .": ibid., 5.

"Kristallnacht was a watershed . . .": Brent, 27.

"Having a relative . . .": ibid.

"'This far exceeds . . .'": Gilbert, 153.

"'We shall take . . .'": ibid.

"Kristallnacht taught the Nazi . . .": ibid., 268.

"The United States took in . . .": ibid., 125.

"'Visas! We began to live . . .'": ibid., 126.

"On 6 July 1938 . . .": ibid., 131.

"bulged with people . . .": Dwork and Van Pelt, 231.

"As the number of Jews . . .": Gilbert, 131–132.

Great Britain: Dwork and Van Pelt, 148.

"With unemployment rampant . . .":, ibid., 144.

"It all took time . . .": Elsley, 33.

"I was left to pace . . .": ibid., 31–32.

"Shop windows were smashed . . .": ibid., 33.

Jewish population in Europe: USHMM, https://www.ushmm.org/wlc
/en/article.php?ModuleId=10005161.

"During the ten months . . ." Gilbert, 268.

CHAPTER EIGHT

"Wave after wave . . .": Speeches in Parliament, November 21, 1938.

"Here is a chance . . .": ibid.

United States' effort: Turner, . . . *And the Policeman Smiled*, 33.

"Even before its life-saving . . .": Gottlieb, 108.

"'Listen, I just got a call . . .'": Wollheim interview, USHMM,
November 18, 1992, 15.

"'I can give you my promise . . .'": Wollheim interview, USHMM,
May 10, 1991, 16.

"There was a big conference . . .": ibid.

"When the hour of departure . . .": ibid., 19.

"I still admire . . .": ibid.

Part Three

"My parents' unspoken decision . . .": Zeller, *When Time Ran Out*, 147.

"I remember dreaming . . .": Eden, 74.

"*Auswanderung*: 'emigration.'": David, *Child of Our Time*, 1.

CHAPTER NINE

"The train was patrolled . . .": Brent, 31.

"Even so, my facial expression . . .": ibid.

Arrival in Harwich: Fast, *Children's Exodus*, 34.

"When my father heard . . .": Elsley, "Without Bitterness," LBI, 37.

"I absolutely hated . . .": ibid., 39.

"We had learned . . .": ibid., 49.

"My parents must have heard . . .": David, "Leaving Germany," 1.

"I had experienced enough . . .": David, *Child of Our Time*, 49.

"I was exhausted . . .": ibid., 52.

"The goodbyes were not tearful . . .": ibid., 53.

"It was dark . . .": David, "Leaving Germany," 1.

VOICES: PARTING

"One day, quite unprepared . . .": Seiden, LBI, 13.

"'I want you to listen . . .'": ibid.

"'It is necessary . . .'": ibid.

"Today on the wall . . .": Koschland, "Bernd Koschland."

"I will never understand . . ."; "How did I feel . . .": ibid.

"The boy had already . . .": Wollheim, USHMM, 1992, 21.

"'Do you take it . . .'": ibid.

"Probably this man . . .": ibid.

"We are told . . .": Korobkin, 19.

"Parents and children clung . . .": ibid., 20.

"Our mother was taking us . . .": Traum, "The Kiddush Cup," USHMM.

"'I have something very important . . .'": Fieldsend, 27.

"We travelled on . . .": ibid., 29–30.

"The station platform . . .": ibid., 31.

Prague operation: Gottlieb, 115.

"When essential papers . . .": Turner, 94–95.

CHAPTER TEN

"From time to time . . .": Rosenbaum, LBI, 2.

"As people would assemble . . .": ibid.

"My mother packed my suitcase . . .": ibid., 5.

"At the first stop . . .": ibid., 6.

"Finally I was the only child . . .": ibid.

"I was confronted with . . .": ibid., 8.

"I look at them . . .": ibid., 12.

"'Oregon is less of a place . . .'": Hsuan, "Fred Rosenbaum . . .".

"'Anybody who got to know . . .'": ibid.

CHAPTER ELEVEN

"always there": Eden, 22.

rock thrown: ibid., 24.

"dangerous, crazy, and evil . . .": ibid., 25.

"A day you get up . . .": ibid., 26.

"Zbaszyn is on the border . . .": ibid., 29.

"There was nothing . . .": ibid., 31.

"You were basically . . .": ibid., 32.

"the agony of lice . . .": ibid.

"The fact that she got . . .": ibid., 35.

"We were actually . . .": ibid., 41.

"But there was also . . .": ibid., 60.

"'Norbert, isn't that the American flag?'": Wollheim, USHMM, 1991, 27

"When we saw that . . .": ibid., 27–28.

Part Four

"You can't chase away . . .": Yosef Itkin in Green, "A Broken Jewish Community."

"Goodness, kindness, love . . .": Winton, Nicholas, interview by Shoah Foundation Institute for Visual History and Education, University of Southern California, July 6, 2015.

"From that last journey . . .": Feuchtwanger, 195–96.

VOICES: LIFE IN A STRANGE LAND

"You picked it up . . .": Eden, 44.

"All of a sudden . . .": ibid.

"I was looking . . .": ibid.

"personal day of independence . . .": Liebenthal, LBI, 7.

"learned to eat fish and chips . . .": ibid., 11.

"War clouds were gathering . . .": ibid.

"Every one of us who got out . . .": ibid., 9.

"Desperately lonely . . .": Heber, "Kindertransport Saved Me from the Nazis."

"Our parents were also . . .": Heber, email to author, October 31, 2017.

"When my mother realized . . .": Heber, "Kindertransport Saved Me from the Nazis."

"There was no question . . .": ibid.

"Dad had the idea . . .": Heber, phone conversation with author, November 7, 2017.

"Be sure to be grateful . . .": ibid.

"I shall always remember . . .": Fieldsend, 31.

"We were seated . . .": Seiden, LBI, 14.

"I put my hands . . .": ibid, 15.

"'Look at these poor girls . . .'": ibid.

"One moment we were . . .": ibid., 17.

"I was yet to learn . . .": ibid.

"It all passed like a dream . . .": Eden, 71.

"The first clear picture . . .": ibid., 72–73.

"We are not left alone . . .": Korobkin, 33.

"The following Monday . . .": Traum, "The Gas Mask," USHMM.

CHAPTER TWELVE

"A bell rings . . .": Brent, 39.

"Some of the little children . . .": Elsley, "Without Bitterness," 40–41.

"This was my first . . .": ibid., 41.

"It is impossible . . .": ibid., 42–43.

"Right from the start . . .": ibid., 43–44.

"I did speak to . . .": ibid., 47.

"I was confused . . .": David, *Child of Our Time*, 53.

"A fantastic vision . . .": David, email to author, October 23, 2018.

"huge, infinite . . .": David, *Child of Our Time*, 55.

"If we were lucky . . .": ibid., 58.

"The Jewish community . . .": ibid.

"In those few months . . .": ibid., 65.

CHAPTER THIRTEEN

"There was an atmosphere . . .": Fieldsend, 36.

"I have to tell you now . . .": BBC "1939: Britain and France . . ."

"About five miles . . .": Van Tijn, "Oh Life of Joy and Sorrow," LBI, 26.

"We ran, and almost . . .": ibid., 27.

"We drove back . . .": ibid.

"Hour after hour . . .": ibid., 28.

CHAPTER FOURTEEN

"'The world war . . .'": Dwork and Van Pelt, 197.

"'clean sweep' to solve . . .": ibid.

OSE: ibid., 208–09.

"anteroom to Auschwitz": ibid., 240.

"'We feverishly notified . . .'": Samuel, *Rescuing the Children*, 83.

American rescue: Dwork and Van Pelt, 236.

OSE efforts: https://childrenofchabannes.org/about-the-ose.

"A child in hiding . . .": Samuel, 99.

"'I'm Jewish, and my name . . .'": ibid., 179.

"'emaciated, sick . . .'": ibid., 186.

"'He was a butcher . . .'": ibid., 185–86.

"'They faced the risk . . .'": ibid., 187.

"'Strongly conscious . . .'": ibid.

VOICES: LOOKING BACK, MOVING FORWARD

"'I'm Mrs. Whyte-Smith . . .'": Korobkin, 38.

"Shefford was the place . . .": ibid., 115.

"I no longer dreamed . . .": ibid., 114.

"It took me some time . . .": ibid., 156.

"What I have learnt . . .": Fieldsend, 174.

"'Dear Boys, when you receive . . .'": ibid., 178–79.

"My mother was really . . .": Eden, 35–36.

"Even a bullet . . .": ibid., 36–37.

"Any mass communication . . .": ibid., 82.

"When the photograph . . .": Traum, "Vienna, Chanukah, 1938," USHMM.

"It was my father's . . .": Traum, "The Kiddush Cup," USHMM.

"'He believed he might . . .'": Zürndorfer, 182.

"What did I feel . . .": Reich, *The Boy in the Statue*, 29.

"By making me part . . .": ibid., 33.

"My instinct has always . . .": ibid., 28.

"How could we not feel happy . . .": Seiden, LBI, 32.

"It was strange that after dreaming . . .": ibid., 54.

"showing their happiness . . .": ibid.

POSTSCRIPT

"The world today . . .": David, *Child of Our Time*, 1.

"I did not think . . .": Elsley, "Without Bitterness," LBI, 1.

"I have succeeded . . .": Brent, 293.

"'Beloved child . . .'": Elsley, "Without Bitterness," LBI, 51–52.

"It is a sad fact . . .": Elsley, *A Chance in Six Million*, 123.

"Until war was declared . . .": Brent, 69.

"the all-important and ominous . . .": ibid., 73.

"I have in my bedroom . . .": ibid., 254–55.

"Looking back on this . . .": Brent, email to author, October 24, 2018.

"to be more compassionate . . .": Brent, 292.

"The war continued . . .": David, *Child of Our Time*, 116.

"I was afraid . . .": ibid., 117.

"My parents had been expelled . . .": David, email to author, September 30, 2018.

"my parents never mentioned . . .": David, *Child of Our Time*, 123.

orange: David, email to author, August 17, 2018.

"'I am thinking . . .'": David, *Child of Our Time*, 142.

"I felt I had a useful role . . .": David, "Readings in German Schools," 4.

"As with other survivors . . .": ibid., 170.

"I once read . . .": Neuberger, W., *Dark Clouds Don't Stay Forever*, 220.

"Here are my final thoughts . . .": Koschland.

PHOTOGRAPH PERMISSIONS

Photos ©: ii-iii: United States Holocaust Memorial Museum, courtesy of Instytut Pamieci Narodowej; vi: Courtesy of The Wiener Library; xi: United States Holocaust Memorial Museum, courtesy of James Sanders; xiii: BHVP/Roger-Viollet; xx: United States Holocaust Memorial Museum, courtesy of Margot Stern Loewenberg; xxiv-1: Associated Press/AP Images; 2, 12, 13, 14: Photograph from the Ruth David collection at the UK National Holocaust Centre and Museum; 21: United States Holocaust Memorial Museum, courtesy of George Fogelson; 22: United States Holocaust Memorial Museum, courtesy of Paul Peter and Lucie Porges; 23: United States Holocaust Memorial Museum, courtesy of Berta Rosenheim Hertz; 26: Courtesy of the family of Hedi Ballantyne Stohr; 31: Imperial War Museum; 34, 35: Library of Congress; 37: Bayerische Staatsbibliothek; 38, 41: Library of Congress; 46: United States Holocaust Memorial Museum, courtesy of Dottie Bennett; 47: United States Holocaust Memorial Museum, courtesy of Liese Fischer; 48, 51: Library of Congress; 54, 56, 57, 58: United States Holocaust Memorial Museum, courtesy of National Archives and Records Administration; 59: Harry Harris/AP Images; 67, 69: Library of Congress; 78: Bayerische

Staatsbibliothek; 88-89: National Archives and Records Administration; 93: United States Holocaust Memorial Museum, courtesy of Lilli Eckstein Stern; 96-97: United States Holocaust Memorial Museum, courtesy of Jewish Community of Giessen; 105: bpk Bildagentur/Art Resource, NY; 109: United States Holocaust Memorial Museum, courtesy of Instytut Pamieci Narodowej; 112: United States Holocaust Memorial Museum, courtesy of Trudy Isenberg; 116: Leo Baeck Institute; 118, 119: United States Holocaust Memorial Museum, courtesy of Leo Goldberger; 122: United States Holocaust Memorial Museum, courtesy of National Archives and Records Administration; 126: bpk Bildagentur/ Karl H. Paulmann/Art Resource, NY; 127: Leo Baeck Institute; 129: United States Holocaust Memorial Museum, courtesy of Lydia Chagoll; 131: United States Holocaust Memorial Museum, courtesy of Robert A. Schmuhl; 144: United States Holocaust Memorial Museum, courtesy of Eva Rosenbaum Abraham-Podietz; 150-151: United States Holocaust Memorial Museum, courtesy of Bea Siegel Green; 155: Courtesy of The Wiener Library; 157: United States Holocaust Memorial Museum, courtesy of Frances Rose; 160: United States Holocaust Memorial Museum, courtesy of Lydia Chagoll; 162: Courtesy of The Wiener Library; 164: AF archive/Alamy Stock Photo; 173: Yad Vashem; 179: United States Holocaust Memorial Museum, courtesy of Henry Schmelzer; 182: National Digital Archives of Poland; 190-191: National Archives and Records Administration; 195:

Associated Press/AP Images; 199: Sueddeutsche Zeitung Photo/Alamy Stock Photo; 208: Courtesy of The Wiener Library; 212: United States Holocaust Memorial Museum, courtesy of National Archives and Records Administration; 224, 226: Associated Press/AP Images; 235: John Fieldsend; 244: United States Holocaust Memorial Museum, courtesy of Alfred Buechler; 247: Courtesy of Dr. Judy Elsley; 253: Photograph from the Ruth David collection at the UK National Holocaust Centre and Museum; 256: Bernd Kocschland.

INDEX

Note: Page numbers in *italics* refer to illustrations.

ACKNOWLEDGMENTS

We Had to Be Brave is, in many ways, the most difficult and rewarding book I've ever written. The subject matter has torn at my heart. As I write these words in the fall of 2018, we are commemorating the eightieth anniversary of Kristallnacht; at the same time, on October 27, the United States suffered the worst anti-Semitic attack in its history with the killing of eleven innocent people in a synagogue in Pittsburgh, Pennsylvania. In these turbulent times, as I've researched and written about the experiences of children in 1930s Germany, what has sustained me most is being in touch with Kindertransport survivors themselves. Thank you.

Many people have given so generously of their time in this project. I hope I don't miss anyone here.

My editor, the extraordinary Lisa Sandell, has once again brought her intelligence, compassion, and wisdom to bear in helping to make this book better. Lisa, her amazing husband, Liel Leibovitz, and their equally amazing children, Lily and Hudson, are my home away from home whenever I visit New York City.

Thanks to my agent, Steven Malk, who puts up with my late-night emails. I'd also like to thank everyone on the Scholastic team. You might not see their names on book jackets, but they work tirelessly to get books into the hands of young readers. Thank you Lori Benton, Ellie Berger, David Levithan, Olivia Valcarce, Keirsten Geise, Becky Terhune, Jael Fogle, Erica Ferguson, Cian O'Day, Emily Teresa, (the incomparable) Lizette Serrano, Emily Heddleson, Jasmine Miranda, Matthew Poulter, Danielle Yadao, Rachel Feld, Tracy van Straaten, Amy Goppert, Lauren Donovan, Shannon Pender, Julia Eisler, Robin Hoffman, Laura Beets and the entire Book Fairs team, and many others—including, of course Mr. John Schu. Thank you!

Now, to those who helped me bring these stories to life. I am immensely grateful to Professor Leslie Baruch Brent, Ruth Oppenheimer David, and Judy Elsley, without whom this book could not have been written. Their courage, generosity of spirit, and commitment to social justice is an inspiration. Leslie and Ruth put up with my many emails; Judy, Lisa, and I endured an agony of anticipation over precious photographs almost lost en route. Thanks also to Michael Simonson, archivist and registrar at the Leo Baeck Institute in New York, for agreeing to read the manuscript and correct errors, and also for enabling me to use memoirs and first-person accounts from the Leo Baeck archives.

Staff members from a number of organizations and museums helped me connect with survivors and make use of oral histories and memoirs. Thanks to Susan Harrod of the Association of Jewish Refugees; Anne LeVant Prahl and Becca Biggs at the Oregon Jewish Museum and Center for Holocaust Education; Kate Sinclair at the National

Holocaust Centre and Museum; and Georgiana Gomez at the USC Shoah Foundation: The Institute for Visual History and Education. Thanks also to the staff of the United States Holocaust Memorial Museum.

I am grateful to Irene Reti for permission to quote from Thea Feliks Eden's *A Transported Life: Memories of Kindertransport*.

The following individuals were generous in answering questions via email, phone, and in person, and also allowing me to use previously published accounts and memoirs. And, even though I could not fit all their stories into the text, their responses were immensely helpful. Thank you to Ruth Barnett, Evelyn Vera Crowe, John Fieldsend, Harry Heber, Frieda Korobkin, Rabbi Daniel Korobkin, Bernd Koschland, Sir Erich Reich, Dorothea Shefer-Vanson, Bronia Snow, Harry Stevens, and Werner Neuburger. A special thanks to Marian Walter of Eugene, Oregon, for welcoming me into her home and sharing her story and providing valuable resources on the Kindertransport as well. In addition, every effort was made to contact publishers for text permissions.

Finally, to my friends, thank you. And to my family—Andy, Dimitri, Rebekah, and Eric—I love you more than anything.

One last thought. As I write this, my grandson, Oliver Sawyer, is only two—not yet old enough to read this book. I hope that in ten years, when he can, he does so in a world that has committed to using the best of ourselves to protect the planet; a place where human ingenuity and creativity help to make life better for people in poverty and solve complex problems like global climate change. I hope that what happened to the people in this book will seem to belong to a distant past.

Yet I hope he will never forget. I hope he will think of them.

ABOUT THE AUTHOR

Deborah Hopkinson is an award-winning author of picture books, middle-grade fiction, and nonfiction. Her nonfiction titles include *Titanic: Voices from the Disaster*, a Sibert Medal Honor Book and YALSA Award for Excellence in Nonfiction finalist; *Courage & Defiance: Stories of Spies, Saboteurs, and Survivors in World War II Denmark*, a Sydney Taylor Notable Book, an NCTE Orbis Pictus Recommended Book, and a winner of the Oregon Book Award and Oregon Spirit Award; *Dive! World War II Stories of Sailors & Submarines in the Pacific*, which was named an NCTE Orbis Pictus Recommended Book and Oregon Spirit Award Honor Book; and, most recently, *D-Day: The World War II Invasion That Changed History*.

Deborah lives with her family near Portland, Oregon. You can visit her online at deborahhopkinson.com and follow her on Twitter @Deborahopkinson and Instagram @deborah_hopkinson.